WHAT EVERY

NEEDS TO KNOW

WHAT EVERY

Bride

NEEDS TO KNOW

THE MOST IMPORTANT YEAR

IN A WOMAN'S LIFE

SUSAN DEVRIES _&_ BOBBIE WOLGEMUTH

ZONDERVAN®

ZONDERVAN.com/
AUTHORTRACKER
follow your favorite authors

ZONDERVAN

What Every Bride Needs to Know
Copyright © 2012 by Susan DeVries and Barbara J. Wolgemuth
Revised and expanded from *The Most Important Year in a Woman's Life*.
Copyright © 2003 by Susan DeVries and Barbara J. Wolgemuth.

This title is also available as a Zondervan ebook.
Visit www.zondervan.com/ebooks.

This title is also available in a Zondervan audio edition.
Visit www.zondervan.com/fm.

Requests for information should be addressed to:

Zondervan, *Grand Rapids, Michigan 49530*

ISBN 978-0-310-31356-4

Published in association with the literary agency of Ann Spangler & Company, 1420
Pontiac Road SE, Grand Rapids, MI 49506.

Cover photography: Paul Shippert Photography
Interior design: Cindy Davis
TRADE decoration: IKEA

Printed in the United States of America

12 13 14 15 16 17 18 19 /DCI/ 20 19 18 17 16 15 14 13 12 11 10 9 8 7 6 5 4 3 2 1

Contents

Introduction

Almost twenty-five years ago Steve and Mary Lee Bartlett became my husband Mark's first premarital counseling experiment. In spite of the fact that Mark was definitely "making it up as he went along," this young couple seemed to enjoy their meetings with him immensely. They laughed, they dreamed, they talked about all the hot topics.

And now, more than a couple of decades later, the Bartletts have become such dear friends that, when we began to work on this book, it was only natural that they would be among the first we'd turn to for input. I asked Mary Lee to assess how prepared she felt for her first year of marriage, and I'll never forget her answer: "We had a great time in our premarital counseling, but I just wish someone had told me how hard it was going to be."

And now, after helping nearly two hundred couples prepare for their marriages—sometimes Mark and I together, other times just Mark by himself—we're sure that Mary Lee is not alone. In fact, research is now confirming how very normal it is for a new bride to be surprised by the difficulty of that first year. One researcher noted that as many as 90 percent of brides surveyed reported experiencing some level of depression during their first year of marriage.[1] Another researcher found that *every* woman she interviewed described an often unexpected feeling of disappointment in the first year after the wedding.[2]

Though we've known many brides who haven't had this kind of experience, the let-down feeling is, of course, natural. A wedding is such an incredible high in a woman's life that just about anything that comes after it is likely to pale in comparison. For some, the post-wedding blues are enough to convince them that they've just made the greatest mistake of their lives. Others feel duped, having believed that Mr. Right would bring automatic satisfaction. And still others enter marriage with a relationship suffering from malnutrition, having poured so much energy into the wedding that the relationship has been left starving for attention.

If you are like most brides, you're longing for a guide to help you navigate the unexpected unsettledness you may be feeling and to help you invest strategically in what we'll be calling the "wet cement year" of your marriage.

Who Are These People and What Are They Trying to Do?

My dear friend Bobbie Wolgemuth and I are excited to share with you some marvelous principles for building an exceptional marriage. But I first want to introduce you to our husbands, Mark DeVries and Robert Wolgemuth—the authors of the companion book, *What Every Groom Needs to Know*.

The Wolgemuth's daughters, Missy and Julie, were in our youth group as they were growing up, and eventually both worked with us in youth ministry. And so it was only natural that they would ask Mark—their youth pastor—to do their premarital counseling and perform their wedding ceremonies. Soon after their weddings the idea of a book came up. Having experienced from a whole different perspective what a powerful influence the right kinds of words can have on a couple starting out, Robert and Bobbie invited us to join them in creating a resource to fortify couples in their first year of marriage.

I want to be clear from the outset that these books are the result of the collaborative effort of the four of us. In one sense, we are four authors of both books. But for the sake of clarity, we have chosen to write each book in only one voice. In this book, you will hear my voice throughout; in *What Every Groom Needs to Know*, you'll hear Robert's. Our dream has been to create books that, by their very format, would bring couples together and would help them become experts at understanding each other.

You'll notice that the chapters of each book have similar titles, but they contain very different material. In this book, we focus on helping you understand your husband and the power of your responsiveness to him. *What Every Groom Needs to Know* is designed to help a husband gain perspective on how he can learn—during this first year—to "bring happiness to the wife he has married," a fascinating biblical phrase you'll learn more about in chapter 1.

What Am I Supposed to Do with This Book?

During the writing, Mark and I met with a group of couples weekly to get their input. What we discovered—delightfully—is that these couples just couldn't seem to stick to evaluating the manuscript. From the very first week, even when the drafts of the chapters were in their infancy and even when the group didn't agree with what we had written, the book's format led them naturally into working on their own marriages.

It's important at the outset that you realize this isn't a book to help you understand "the normal man," because the man you married is undoubtedly far from average. It's a book to help you accomplish your mission of becoming an expert on this one man you have been given as your life partner. Here's a process that can help you apply what you are learning — to the end that you and your spouse will know and enjoy each other more than you've dared to dream:

1. **Feel Free to Sneak:** Among the members of our group, we found that wives had a sneaky habit of reading the men's book. And every now and then, even the most reading-resistant man would snoop around in the women's book, just to see if we were telling the truth.

2. **Ask the Expert:** There will likely be things you read about "men in general" that just aren't true about the man you've married. When you run across those things, ask your husband questions like, "Is this really what you think?" and, "Is this true for you?"

3. **Be the Expert:** Even if you've only been married for a few weeks, your husband may already be confused. You can help him understand and enjoy you more by being warmly responsive to his questions and his attempts to understand your heart.

Is This Stuff Really True?

The stories you're about to read are true, though many of the details are not. The names and the circumstances have been changed to mask the identity of those whose stories we are telling. And at times we've combined the experiences of several couples into a seamless story with entirely different names and circumstances.

We also want to acknowledge that the subtitle *The Most Important Year* is true, of course, for those women who choose to marry. However, if the first year of marriage were the only "most important year," a person of no less stature than Mother Teresa would have missed it. But because you and I *have* chosen marriage, and because the first year of marriage *is* so critical in shaping our futures, we are convinced that nothing conveys the heart of our message quite like *The Most Important Year in a Woman's Life.*

So whether you are preparing for marriage or have been married for thirty days or for thirty years, we invite you to make this next year *the most important year* in your life.

Susan DeVries   *Bobbie Wolgemuth*
Nashville, Tennessee   *Orlando, Florida*

1

The Most Important Year: Reality Check

The first change the woman must adjust to is no longer being a bride.

SHERYL NISSINEN, *THE CONSCIOUS BRIDE*

---

*B*y now I don't have to tell you. If you're looking for information on how to be a bride, you won't have to look far. There are thousands of books, magazines, bridal shows, and Websites—all offering tips and checklists to help the well-organized bride plan her wedding. And since most of these lists start with "twelve months before the wedding," many of us find ourselves way behind before we even get started—and we haven't caught up yet.

In my research, I found lists that seem to cover everything—from picking out the dress to designing a map to the reception. But I couldn't find a single checklist that included the estimated amount of time a bride could expect to spend on these gargantuan to-do lists.

So I put my own calculator to a few of these tasks and came up with my own estimates. Did you know that the typical bride will spend between 150 and 500 hours preparing for her wedding—the equivalent of one to three months working at a full-time job? After the year you've had, you're not surprised, are you?

If you were like most brides, you probably spent an incredible amount of time and energy creating the wedding that would be "just right" for you and your husband—the kind of day you've been dreaming of and planning for since you were a little girl. And now that the special day is over, there's a good chance you're feeling what a lot of women experience, namely, the postmarital blues. I call it "the princess crisis."

A princess is beautiful, fun to be with, romantic, on a quest to win the affection of a charming prince, and surrounded by others who attend to her wants and needs. But after the wedding day, a bride often ceases to see herself as a princess—feeling more like the duty-bound queen—and when the princess becomes the queen, the real work begins.

You may have noticed one other item notoriously absent from the premarital checklists: time allotted to working on your relationship with your future husband. I took out my calculator again to try to determine how much time a typical couple spends before their wedding working on developing the attitudes and skills they'll need to build a great marriage. The diligent couple will go to premarital counseling—usually five hours or so. And the really committed couples will read a book on marriage—say, another ten hours. At best, the average couple will spend ten times more time preparing for the wedding event than for their marriage.

It's not uncommon for a bride, carried along by the rushing torrent of preparing for the wedding day, to neglect her relationship with her fiancé. And it is not uncommon for couples in their first year of marriage, carried along by the rushing momentum of getting established in a new home — often in a new town with new jobs — to neglect their relationship with each other, only to find themselves wondering at the end of the first year what happened to all the love they once felt on their wedding day.

But *you* have picked up this book because you want something more for your marriage. Welcome!

More Than Commitment

The ever-growing stacks of marriage and relationship books at libraries and bookstores give evidence of how intensely people long to make their marriages work. In fact, in the past thirty years there have been more books written on marriage than there were in the previous two thousand years combined. Yet, despite the deluge of resources, we don't have to look far to realize that *great ideas* on marriage, in and of themselves, do not make great marriages.

Some say that marriages fail because of a lack of commitment. Some say the problem is that couples today lack a proper spiritual foundation. Others say the root of the problem is that couples are simply not willing to sacrifice in ways that their parents and grandparents did. But Bobbie and I are convinced that, regardless of the reason, the demise or the success of a marriage can almost always be traced to the first year together.

Here's how it went with Sheila. All her life she had dreamed of being married — of having someone to share life with, someone to walk on the beach with, to dance with, simply to share the stories of the day with. When she met Ted, she knew she had found the man she had been hoping for. He was strong and stable, quietly eager to please her, and he was ambitious. He knew what he wanted out of life, and she liked that.

But shortly after their wedding, Sheila realized that this man of her dreams had the strange habit of leaving her feeling hurt and lonely. She longed for the closeness they had known when they were dating, but so often it seemed as though he was far away—almost unreachable.

Sheila committed herself to working even harder at being a better wife. She tried to be sensitive to Ted's moods and needs, serving him as unselfishly as she knew how. But she found that Ted simply came to expect these things and seldom expressed appreciation for them.

This went on for years, through the birth and growth of their two children. By the time the kids got busy with lives of their own, Sheila's ache returned in full bloom. She tried to talk to Ted about her long-standing disenchantment with their marriage. Ted was preoccupied with his work and chided her for her "lousy sense of timing."

It wasn't long after their twentieth anniversary that Sheila made the decision to do what she had told herself she would never do. When the divorce papers were delivered to Ted, she finally had his undivided attention. Ted tried to talk her out of it, but Sheila was on a mission. Under pressure from close friends, Sheila and Ted went to see a counselor. But the negativity was so strong by this point that, try as they might, Sheila and Ted could never find a solid foothold on which to start over. They said the line—repeated so often by so many—"We tried so hard; we tried *everything*, and nothing worked."

It's not that Ted and Sheila didn't invest in their marriage. The truth is that they invested sacrificially as they tried desperately to make their marriage work. Their investment was enormous. It simply came *too late*.

But the seeds of failure were planted in the first year of the marriage—seeds that over time grew strong enough to corrode their commitment. During that first year, changes could have been made—with minimal effort. But after twenty years of ingrained patterns, even Ted and Sheila's heroic efforts were consumed in a tidal wave of negativity that they felt helpless to stop.

Here's the principle: The early investment in building an exceptional marriage costs a fraction of what it will take to keep a lousy one on life support. The early investment takes less time. It takes less emotional anxiety. Consider the dividends:

- People with satisfying marriages live longer, enjoy better health, and report a much higher level of satisfaction about life in general. In fact, people who stay married, live an average of four years longer than people who don't.[3]
- Forty percent of married couples say they are very happy, compared to 18 percent of those divorced and 22 percent of those never married or of unmarried couples living together.[4]
- Recent statistics show that the average married couple in their fifties has a net worth nearly five times that of the average divorced or single person.[5]
- Divorce dramatically increases the likelihood of early death from strokes, hypertension, respiratory cancer, and intestinal cancer. Astonishingly, being a divorced nonsmoker is only slightly less dangerous than smoking a pack (or more) of cigarettes a day and staying married! (I wonder if divorce summons papers come with the surgeon general's warning).[6]

The Most Important Year

As we began our treasure hunt to find the secrets of building a great marriage, we came across this passage from the Old Testament, buried in the middle of the often ignored book of Deuteronomy. Here, hidden just before the instructions concerning the proper use of millstones when making loan agreements (no kidding), is a single verse that just may make all the difference in the world in your marriage:

> If a man has recently married, he must not be sent to war or have any other duty laid on him. For one year he is to be free to stay at home and bring happiness to the wife he has married.
>
> DEUTERONOMY 24:5

Although the prospects of such a thing may sound hilarious or outrageous to you, take a look at the principles embedded in this verse — principles that just may make your first year of marriage the most important year in your life.

The "Wet Cement Year" Principle — "has recently married"

Have you ever walked down a sidewalk and seen a handprint or someone's name etched into its surface? Think about how much work it took to make those marks and how difficult it would be to change them. Indelible marks are made on your marriage early. They're not very difficult to make, but they're extremely difficult to change.

Scripture is clear that there is — and should be — something undeniably different about the first year of marriage. The implication is that, particularly for a husband, there is a receptivity to change during this year, perhaps as at no other time in his life. We call this "the wet cement year." Once the patterns of the marriage are set, change can and does occur, but it may take something like a jackhammer to bring it about.

Too many women spend the first year of marriage working hard not to make waves, hoping that the little irritants and insensitivities of their husbands will simply go away. But in almost every marriage we've observed, problems not dealt with in the first year simply become larger and more paralyzing as the years go by.

The Slow Learner Principle — "For one year"

Have you ever heard one of these comments come out of a woman's mouth?

- "If he really loved me, he would figure it out."
- "How can he say that he loves me and keep doing the same insensitive things again and again?"
- "If I have to *tell* him what I want, then it doesn't count!"

Consider the contrast between the attitude that lies beneath these comments and the suggestion from the Bible that it will take a man *an entire year of focused effort* to learn how to please his wife. An entire year!

The changes that a couple needs to make (particularly the changes the husband needs to make) *can* be less painful if dealt with in the first year, but they may not come quickly. Our friend Lois was particularly startled at how challenging the first year of her marriage was. Things just fell into place so naturally when she and Andy were dating. But now, it felt as though they were swimming through molasses. Her frustration came primarily because she wasn't prepared. She simply hadn't anticipated how slowly her husband would be able to "figure things out."

Awareness that lasting change will take time can free a wife from having to resort to negative nagging to motivate her husband into change. Being prepared in this way can help her to celebrate the small steps of growth her husband does make as he is learning to "bring happiness" to her.

Let's face facts: Most husbands are clueless when it comes to understanding women. They love their wives and want to see them happy. But they are easily confused about expressing love in a way that truly brings pleasure to their wives. Husbands wonder—

- Is it talking together as you go for a long walk? Or is it taking a short walk together in silence?
- Is it a romantic night together in the bedroom with candles and soft music? Or is it helping with the dishes so she doesn't have to fuss over them in the morning?
- Is it getting flowers once a week? Or is it weeding the garden on Saturday mornings?
- Is it sending a romantic card? Or is it simply putting dirty clothes in the hamper?
- Is it cooking out on the grill at home? Or is it calling ahead to make dinner reservations?
- Is it letting her plan an entire vacation? Or is it planning a surprise getaway without her having to do a thing?

Look closely at the Old Testament passage again. The good news hinted at in this ancient Scripture is that your husband *can*, in fact, learn to understand what brings you pleasure. Your husband is not expected to become a genius when it comes to *women*. He is, though, charged to become the world's greatest expert at understanding what pleases *you!* And to accomplish this, he will need your help.

The Responsive Feedback Principle — "bring happiness to the wife he has married"

Bobbie has a friend who was a first-grade teacher. She told me the story of Zachary, the boy with the unkempt hair. Day after day Zachary came to school with a terminal case of "bed head." *What is this boy's mother thinking?* that teacher wondered.

One day she announced, "Tomorrow is picture day," and then she wrote a note to the children's mothers and sent it home in the kids' backpacks. To her amazement, the next day Zachary walked into the classroom with his hair perfectly combed. *This* was her big chance. Before class began, Zachary made his way toward her desk, and she spoke to him quietly enough that none of the other students could hear. "Wow, Zachary, you'd better get your running shoes on," she said with a twinkle in her eye. "Your hair looks so good that all the girls will be chasing you today!"

She never had to say anything else the rest of the year about Zachary's hair. She didn't need to.

Men are wired a good bit like little Zachary—wired to respond to the positive feedback that comes from the decisions they make. There are few things more powerful a wife can do to motivate her husband than to let him know that his actions and his words are making a difference.

I love the way psychologist Neil Clark Warren makes sense of this process: "My love for another person is strongly related to my love for myself when we are together. If the most potent motivation in my life is to feel good about myself—and I believe it is—then I will love an individual most when she helps me to feel best about myself."[7]

When a wife says, "I like that!" or "That counts for me," her husband feels empowered and motivated and is much more likely to repeat what he did to please her. But a man who believes that he can never satisfy his wife will soon give up trying and invest his energy in places—like his job—where the results are much more clearly seen. Am I suggesting that you fake happiness so your husband can feel good about himself? Not at all. I'm merely saying that one of the greatest gifts you'll ever give him is to *respond* well to the things he *does* do that make you happy. He needs to know that you noticed.

Investing in the Real Journey

In 1845, Sir John Franklin and 138 men set off from England to find a northwest passage to the Pacific Ocean. Their course would take them over the Canadian Arctic.

The ship was well stocked for comfort—a 1,200-volume library, a hand organ programmed to play fifty different melodies, fine china and monogrammed silver place settings, and hand-carved backgammon boards.

But not a single one of the sailors would live to tell his story. For years, no one knew what had happened until an expedition stumbled upon their frozen remains. The ship was found first—frozen solid in the arctic waters of the Canadian north. Apparently, the engines weren't equipped to run in such ominously cold temperatures. And though the ship was outfitted with an auxiliary coal-powered engine, according to the ship's logs, they had no more than twelve days' supply of coal on board. Eventually, the crew was forced to travel by foot.

Years later explorers came upon the remains of the sailors, frozen in tents or beneath the shelter of the single lifeboat they dragged across the ice for over a hundred miles. But it wasn't the gruesome remains that most surprised these explorers. As they looked more closely at the lost sailors, they were amazed to discover brass buttons and silk scarves. These men appeared to have entered their journey more equipped for elegance than for survival.

Sir John Franklin and his crew entered their adventure with enthusiasm. They had the highest levels of commitment. They had a plan and plenty of passion. They even supplied themselves with an abundance of luxuries to make their journey more comfortable. *But they weren't prepared.*

Building a satisfying marriage isn't simply about commitment and passion. It's about being prepared for the winters that are sure to come. Will you enter marriage with enough coal for the reserve engines, or will your attention be fixed on all kinds of wedding-shower trinkets and gadgets—luxuries that promise to make life more comfortable? The most elegant and memorable weddings in the world become useless ornaments unless couples prepare well.

Before you turn the page, make the decision to do the preparations that will cause this to be the most important year in your life.

2
Needs: Dare to Dream the Impossible

Being helpful to each other will do far more for the strength and passion of your marriage than a two-week Bahamas getaway.

JOHN GOTTMAN, *THE SEVEN PRINCIPLES FOR MAKING MARRIAGE WORK*

———◆◆◆———

*I*magine this scene:

It's a Saturday, and you had to work all day. Your husband had the day off. It's 7:00 P.M. when you finally drag yourself through the doorway. But when you come in, you instantly notice something different about your home. No stray papers. The kitchen is immaculate.

In the dining room, you see the flicker of candles. And something smells tantalizing. Over the mellow sounds of your favorite music playing in the background, you call out, "Honey? What's going on? Is someone coming over tonight?"

Your tuxedoed husband appears from around the corner and says playfully, "Welcome, madam. We *are* expecting a very important guest—and she has just arrived. As we put the finishing touches on your dinner, I hope you'll come and make yourself comfortable in our lounge."

As you raise a skeptical eyebrow, this man of yours leads you to a comfortable chair, next to which he has strategically placed your favorite drink and that magazine or catalog you never have time to read.

You pinch yourself to make sure you're not dreaming . . .

Mark and I have shared this imaginary scenario with enough groups of married couples to know what to expect: the rolling eyes, the snickers of laughter, comments like, "Yeah right!" or "Come on, be realistic!" or "The closest I'll ever get to that story IS in my dreams."

But before you move this book to the fantasy section of your home library, I want to ask you to consider the possibility that having a husband who cherishes you with this kind—or more appropriately, "your kind"—of extravagance and creativity is not only possible, it's actually crucial if you are to have the marriage you always dreamed of.

And I've got news for you: There really *are* wives who experience this dream on a regular basis—not every night of course, maybe not even every month, but frequently enough to make them shake their heads and wonder how God could be so good as to give them the husbands they have. There is more involved here than just dumb luck. This kind of treatment never happens accidentally but only to couples who have intentionally chosen to find joy in meeting each other's needs in extravagant and surprising ways.

Helping Your Husband Succeed

So what would make your husband treat you this way? Remember that in a healthy marriage a husband finds great joy in bringing pleasure to his wife. One of the most important things you can do during the first year of your marriage is help your husband succeed in doing just that. And to help him succeed, you'll need to develop three specific skills:

1. Know your own needs well enough to understand what your husband can do to bring you pleasure.
2. Express those needs to your husband clearly, specifically, and winsomely.
3. Cherish your husband with as much creativity as you hope he will use cherishing you.

Know Your Own Needs: Why Most Wives Miss the Party

Mark and I recently worked through our standard premarital preparation process with an exceptional young couple. They had convictions about their plans for Bible study and prayer times together after the wedding. They were committed to reading marriage books together. They even agreed to have weekly financial meetings to head off any potential conflicts over money. This was a couple with an uncanny commitment to having an incredible marriage.

In the final session, though, we recognized a pattern that had the potential to severely limit the joy these two would experience in their marriage. We were on the topic of "great sex in marriage." Within thirty seconds, the young bride-to-be, obviously a bit uncomfortable with my candor, interrupted me, "I've just decided that I'm going to leave everything in this area up to John [her fiancé]. That's really his department."

I answered her slowly, "No, Marcia, I'm afraid that's *your* department."

The bride-to-be was confused. As her brows furrowed, she asked, "What do you mean?"

I explained that very few wives I had talked to were truly satisfied with the sexual side of their marriages. I explained that very few men ever actually "figure out" what truly pleases their wives sexually, *unless* their wives teach them. I explained how brides who see sex as "their husbands' department" eventually wind up approaching sex as a chore—an obligation she fulfills for his sake rather than a playful, deeply satisfying experience that she enjoys as much—if not more—than her husband.

Finally, I explained that wives who leave sex as their husbands' department usually become experts at "avoidance strategies." Sometimes it's evening headaches; other nights it's late meetings at church; and still other times, it's "unselfishly" tidying up the house at night until the husband is asleep.

I knew we had this bride-to-be's attention. She said, "That is *not* what I want! But what do you mean when you say it's *my* department?"

Mark explained, "It's not just your sexual needs that are your department. Sex is just an example of a place where it's common for a wife to be completely out of touch with her own needs. It's just that if *you* don't know your needs, it's pretty unlikely that your husband will somehow stumble into figuring out how to meet them. For a woman to expect her husband to know her needs better than she does herself—whether it relates to sex or to sandwiches—simply sets both of them up for frustration."

Circling back to the original topic, I affirmed, "It *is* your responsibility to discover enough about yourself over this next year that you become an expert on what your husband can do to satisfy you sexually. As awkward as it may seem right now, that *is* your department."

Let's face it: Knowing our own needs may not feel natural. Many of us grew up with the subtle message that we are not supposed to have needs of our own. We have heard the message loud and clear: "Work harder. Serve more. Stop focusing so much on yourself." Though ignoring our own needs may feel natural or seem unselfish, the truth is that living this way can actually *prevent* our husbands from doing the very thing we long for them to do, namely, to cherish us.

Ask for What You Need: Why Most Husbands Stay Clueless

Some time ago, my friend Cathryn told her husband, Billy, about a surprise birthday party one of his friends had thrown for his wife. Cathryn told Billy how excited her friend was and how fun the whole idea sounded. She talked with great enthusiasm about how special her friend felt that her husband had gone to all that trouble.

In a few months, Cathryn's thirtieth birthday came. Billy took her out for an expensive dinner and gave her a very nice gift, and then the two of them came home for a quiet evening together. But by bedtime, Billy could tell that there was something wrong.

He asked, "Are you okay? You look a little down."

Eventually, she admitted, "I thought you were going to throw a surprise party for me this year!"

Billy asked (with typical male sensitivity), "If you wanted a surprise party, why didn't you ask for one?"

Cathryn shot back, "I did!"

What was Billy's mistake? He assumed that when his bride was talking about *her friend's* surprise party that she was really talking about *her friend's* surprise party. What you and I both know is that she was talking about what she wanted from her husband. Cathryn made the common mistake of forgetting what gender her husband was.

I love my husband. He is a marvelous man. He presents seminars, counsels couples, and writes books about marriage. But there are times when he just doesn't get it. And if I hadn't learned over the years to ask clearly for what I need from him, he would still be scratching his head and trying to figure me out.

When we ask couples in trouble what they would love to see happen in their marriages, we often receive detailed lists of what they don't like about their spouse's behavior. But seldom does this kind of negative response help couples get what they deeply long for from each other. Moving from vague criticisms to expressions of specific needs can actually transform a marriage.

For example, a wife might say to her husband, "I want you to be less selfish." The husband might naturally respond with a list of all the unselfish things he's already doing—"I mow the lawn. I'm nice to your mother. I pay all the bills." But her concern about selfishness is much more specific. Her husband has a habit of making plans in the evening without letting her know, so she winds up cooking a nice dinner he ends up not eating or appreciating.

When you find yourself nagging your husband, it's almost always because there is something you want from him that you're not getting. And often it's a sign that you haven't clearly asked for what you need.

Remember Aladdin and his magic lamp? Imagine the genie asking you to make your first wish.

You respond, "I'd like more money."

He tells you to reach into your pocket. You find a quarter, just as the genie says, "How about your next wish?"

You would be thinking, "That's *not* what I meant!"

Your husband is not a genie, but like this genie, he may at times give you exactly what you have "asked for," only to learn later that what he gave you was *not* what you meant. Consider the difference between these two very different requests for the same need:

- "You never touch me anymore."
- "Would you rub my back tonight for about five minutes?"

Your husband will likely see the first request as a criticism and assume you must be talking about sex. With regard to the second request, you are much more likely to get your back massage, and your husband is much more likely to feel as though he's succeeded in loving you.

When we talk to husbands, we hear an almost unanimous chorus: "If I could just figure out what she wanted, I would do it. But it seems like no matter what I do, it's not the right thing." Am I suggesting that *every time* you ask directly for what you need from your husband he will say yes? Of course not. What I am saying is that wives who ask directly for what they need are *always* more likely to have these needs met by their husbands than if they hadn't asked at all. Hockey star Wayne Gretzky is right: "We miss 100 percent of the shots we never take."

One final tip about asking: In addition to being specific and clear about what you need from your husband, he'll be much more receptive if your requests are given winsomely. Clear and specific requests can easily be negated by a spirit of bitterness or anger on the part of the one doing the asking.

Learn to Cherish Your Husband: He's Not Asking for Much

If you hope to create a marriage in which you and your husband cherish each other extravagantly and creatively, the third skill you'll need to learn is the skill of knowing and meeting your husband's needs with the same playful intentionality you hope he uses in trying to meet yours. Without this step, the first two skills can easily be viewed by your husband as demanding and unrealistic neediness on your part.

How do you discover what your husband desires most from you? You might assume that the easiest way to find the answer is simply to ask him. It can't hurt. But if you get less than a clear, specific response, don't be surprised. Willard Harley's book *His Needs, Her Needs* was a real eye-opener for me. Dr. Harley says that the most effective currency a husband and wife have for communicating love to each other is that of *meeting each other's needs*. His theory, after counseling hundreds of couples, is that men and women each have a set of five very different primary needs. Here are the ones he suggests your husband needs from you:[8]

1. sexual fulfillment
2. recreational companionship
3. an attractive spouse
4. domestic support
5. admiration

I'm not saying that these are the needs that all men have or ought to have. I simply offer this list as a starting point for you on your journey toward discovering the needs of this man you have married. So take this list to him, and see if he agrees. If he doesn't, be sure to find out what needs he *does* have.

Another possibility is to ask a few playful discovery questions such as—

- What one thing could I do for you today that would let you know how much I love you?
- If you knew I would say yes, what one thing would you ask me to do with you or for you?
- What would be your perfect night at home? Be as detailed as possible.

Now this is where the fun comes in. Whatever your husband asks, surprise him by doing it sometime in the next week. And add a little extra to it. If he asks for meat loaf and mashed potatoes for dinner, prepare his favorite dessert as well. If he asks you to be more available sexually, initiate an intimate encounter once a week.

It's funny. If asked, most Christian wives would say they'd be willing to die for their husbands. But some of these same wives view it as a grand imposition to demonstrate love in the little ways that meet their husbands' needs, such as being happy with them, enthusiastically greeting them at the door, or flirting back with them.

If husbands of these women ever dare to say that they don't feel much love coming from their wives, these wives are quick to point to all the things they're doing to show love:

- "Haven't I taken care of the house, done your laundry, and fed the dog?"
- "Didn't I buy you that cool golf shirt?"
- "Don't I pray for you every day?"

Clearly, it's not wrong for a wife to do these things for her husband. The problem comes when she assumes that, because she does the things *she* thinks ought to meet his needs, his needs are truly being met. A wife who "unselfishly" focuses her time on the things she wants to do for her husband, while ignoring the things that matter most to him, should not confuse what she is doing with love. Your charge is to outdo one another in showing love (see Romans 12:10).

The **Yes** Spiral

In premarital counseling, we describe this process of meeting each other's needs as the *Yes Spiral*. The more that couples tap into this widening upward spiral, the more likely they are to experience the kind of marriages they've dreamed of. We call it the *Yes Spiral* because it all begins with a willingness to say yes to the request—spoken or unspoken—to meet the needs of your spouse.

Let's take a look at the widening spiral that comes when a husband and wife learn to live with a resounding, mutual *Yes!* toward each other. Here's how the spiral can begin on an ordinary day when you arrive home from work:

> *You:* "Hi, sweetie, I'm home." No response from your husband. "How 'bout a little welcome parade for the princess of the castle?"
>
> *Your Husband:* "I'm sorry. I was caught up in getting my report done." He hugs you and looks into your eyes. "I have a huge favor to ask. I hate to ask you to go out after you just got in, but I was printing out this report that has to be turned in tonight, and I realized I need a few things from Officeland. Could you run over there and get them for me?"
>
> *You:* "Sure. What do I need to get?"
>
> *Your Husband:* "You're the best, honey. Here's the list."
>
> *You:* "Hey, if you get the chance while I'm out, could you call your folks to see when we need

to pick up that package? I couldn't get ahold of them earlier today."

Your Husband: "No problem." You turn to go, and he stops you. "Hey, you're pretty incredible, you know that?"

You: "Come here, you!"

You wrap him in your arms.

Your Husband: "Hey, princess, if you hurry back, I may just have to take you out to dinner tonight." As you leave, he's shaking his head, smiling and saying quietly to himself, "You amaze me!"

A simple—almost silly—conversation, but did you observe how many times you and your husband said yes to each other in this quick exchange?

1. He said yes to your request for a warm greeting, even though he was consumed with his project.
2. You said yes to his request to make an unplanned trip to the store, even though getting back in the car was the last thing you wanted to do.
3. He said yes to your request to call his parents about the package.
4. You both said yes to each other's need for appreciation and affirmation.

With each yes—in words, actions, or attitudes—the spiral widens, and the two of you feel freer together, more willing to serve each other, more willing to creatively meet each other's needs.

But when the positive responses are replaced by negative ones, the spiral becomes tighter and tighter. You both feel more trapped, less willing to serve, more like you're locked in a room with a porcupine. Here's how the conversation, carried out differently, creates a constricting spiral:

> *Wife:* "Hi, sweetie, I'm home." No response from your husband. "How 'bout a little welcome parade for the princess of the castle?"
>
> *Husband (shouting from his office):* "I'm sorry. I was just trying to finish this report for tonight. Hey, I hate to ask you to go out after you've just got in, but I really need some stuff from Office-land so I can get this report done and turned in. Could you run to the store and get it for me?"
>
> *Wife:* "You've had all day. You've been out three times. Why didn't you pick up what you needed when you were out?"
>
> *Husband:* "I didn't realize I needed it until I got to this point in the report. I've had a few other things on my mind, you know. Here's the list."
>
> *Wife (handing the list back):* "You'll just have to take care of it yourself. I am *not* going out again. Not after the day I've had! Where's the mail? Do I have any messages? Did you call your parents about when we need to pick up that package?"
>
> *Husband:* "I distinctly remember you telling me you were going to do it. You know, I can't do everything! I have a job, too, you know."
>
> *Wife:* "Fine! I don't care if we get the package or not."
>
> *Husband (through clenched teeth):* "So did you learn this little attitude in your marriage class at church?"

Wife: "Now that was a cheap shot, and you know it."

Husband (getting up): "Excuse me, but I need to go to the store. Don't worry about me joining you for dinner tonight. Now that I've got to make this extra trip out, I'll have to work straight through dinner to get this report turned in on time." He stalks away, fuming. "You amaze me!"

Did you notice how easily each of them became less and less willing to say yes. Once the downward spiral begins, it takes increasing amounts of energy to move against the negative inertia.

Consider for just a minute the investment of energy in these two conversations. The first feels like a walk down lovers' lane compared to the second, doesn't it? But notice that the first conversation required an up-front, against-the-grain willingness to meet each other's needs, even when it wasn't convenient.

I am sometimes asked, "What if I don't really *feel* like doing what my husband needs me to do? You're not suggesting I do it anyway, even though my heart isn't in it, are you?" Well, yes, that's exactly what I'm suggesting!

You find an example of this very behavior in the first dialogue. In the second, the couple simply did and said what they felt like saying and doing. Love doesn't mean we'll always feel like demonstrating love; it means choosing to demonstrate love—even when we don't feel like it.

Suppose a mother waited to "feel like it" before she changed her baby's diaper. Her child could wallow in his own mess for a long time before she ever "felt like it." Even though her heart may not be in it, she changes the diaper anyway. Why? Because she loves the child, even though she may not *feel* particularly loving at the time.

The decision to meet each other's needs is not primarily about saying the right things. It's not about learning how to perfectly imitate dialogue number one. Rather, it is about possessing an eagerness to say yes to your husband's needs. Since you are, in reality, "one flesh" with your husband, when you meet *his* needs, in some mysterious way you are meeting *your own* needs as well.

But even though you know how important it is to meet each other's needs, there will be times when you're simply not capable. That's okay. In the next chapter, I have some good news for you.

3

Spiritual Unity: More Than Meets the Eye

As man was incomplete in the Genesis story, so man and woman are incomplete from an ultimate, divine perspective. We believe every human couple needs a critical third partner, and that third factor is God.

DEAN BORGMAN, *WHEN KUMBAYA IS NOT ENOUGH*

———◆✦◆———

We knew Brad and Francine quite well by the time they finished their premarital meetings with us. Both had fiery personalities and shared a common heart for God. As we spent time together, Mark cautioned them that their intense approach to life could make for some challenging and uncomfortable conflict, though I'm not sure they believed him.

By the end of their first year of marriage, they had learned each other's hot buttons and punched them with pugnacious regularity. On most days, their anger simmered below the surface, but at times it boiled over with a destructive harshness that frightened both of them.

Not long ago, we had dinner with Francine and Brad. Shaking her head and laughing, Francine said to us, "We would have easily divorced a hundred times in that first year."

Surprised and curious, I asked, "Why did you stay together?"

They answered in playful unison, "God!"

They would tell you that it wasn't that God stepped in, snapped his fingers, and suddenly made them get along. Rather, it was their common loyalty to the God whom they both deeply loved that gave them the heart to stay together, even when they didn't much care for each other and staying together was the last thing they *felt* like doing.

The Third Partner

Because of the commitment Brad and Francine had made to honor God, they did not simply resign themselves to tolerating a lifetime of mutual annoyance. They were motivated to change the ingrained patterns of resistance toward each other that could have pulled them apart. The good news is that you and your husband cannot both move closer to God without moving closer to each other. I picture it like this:

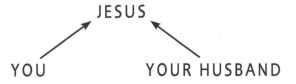

You may recall that men tend to build intimacy best when they are focused on a third object—whether it's football, food, or a military mission. And the greater the third object, the deeper and stronger their bond. Some theologians refer to this phenomenon as the "transcendent third"—something outside two people that draws them together. A husband and wife who have Titans football as their "transcendent third" are brought together by their common football allegiance. But we'd hardly expect this shared fan loyalty alone to enable a couple to overcome even minimal obstacles in their relationship. They need something bigger.

For some couples, children become the "transcendent third" that gives them leverage to work through annoying behaviors in each other. But focusing on children as the highest "transcendent third" can mask the absence of a true spiritual connection in the marriage. Again, they need something bigger.

But when a husband and wife are each actively seeking God—moving toward *the* "Transcendent Third"—they pursue One who is so engaging, so captivating, so transforming, so supremely good, that loyalty to him stabilizes and engulfs all other loyalties. God is big enough.

Encouraging Your Husband to Grow

With a voice as deep as the Grand Canyon, Doug was a man's man. He had spent the early years of his marriage working in and around the coal mines of western Canada. And though he had traveled as a young boy with his minister-father, Doug considered God irrelevant.

Doug didn't resist when his wife offered to take their young children to church. He was happy to let her. What harm could it do? *After all,* he thought, *kids need good moral input.*

This arrangement worked fine for Doug and Jan until the children became too much for her to handle at the church service. One day she came home and said, "You have to start coming to church with me. I just can't handle these kids all by myself."

To Doug's credit, he agreed and began attending church as the bouncer for his elementary-age kids—and that's when his world turned upside down.

Doug never expected to find "real men" at church; he expected only "pansies." What he found were rock-solid men, just like he thought he was. And so, when one of the men from church asked Doug if he wanted to join their group for a little road trip, an event sponsored by a group he'd never heard of—a group called Promise Keepers—Doug said, "Sure."

In Jan's words, when Doug came back from that event, "everything changed." An encounter with God did something for Doug that Jan could never do. Her husband came home with a commitment to provide spiritual leadership in their home and with a renewed love for her and the children.

It might be easy to assume that Jan had little to do with the transformation in her husband's life, but I don't buy it for a second. What Jan did was to create a climate of such receptivity in her husband that, once he encountered God himself, he became an entirely different man.

It is not unusual for a wife to be further along spiritually than her husband. But there is a certain style, a particular attitude, common to wives who effectively encourage their husbands to move from spiritual apathy to spiritual passion. We've joyfully observed many husbands who have been wooed and won by the irresistible spiritual influence of their wives. These women don't try to argue their husbands into spiritual depth. They don't berate them for not being spiritual enough. They don't claim to know the answers to all the questions. They don't try to trick their husbands into "witnessing ambushes" cleverly disguised as dinner parties at the homes of Christian friends.

No, there is something refreshing about the wild honesty of these women's faith. Their husbands are attracted to the vitality of a woman whose love for God infects every part of her with a deeper passion, so that she wants to be more patient, more understanding, more winsome, and able to laugh at herself more readily.

What spiritually resistant men usually fear is not that their wives will become too bright and too alive by knowing Jesus but that they will become too boring, one-dimensional, and adventureless. So if your husband is put off by God or by the church, find out what will turn him on spiritually—and wait for your wooing witness to have its effect.

Honor and Respect Your Husband's Pursuit of God

Even if you grew up going to church every time the doors were open, you may be able to remember a time when talking about spiritual things felt uncomfortable. Whether it was being put on the spot when someone asked you to pray or responding to a "simple" Sunday school question in broad daylight, you felt embarrassed. Your husband may feel this "public spiritual insecurity" more acutely than you ever felt it.

Remember that spiritual unity does not mean spiritual uniformity. And one of the first ways to encourage your husband to grow in his own relationship with Jesus is to honor his style of living out his faith. It's refreshing to see a man emboldened to take the next step spiritually as the result of a simple, encouraging comment from his wife, such as, "It's great the way you help people—seeing things that need to be done and just doing them," or, "I love the way you cut through all the clutter and get to the real issue when we talk about spiritual things." Catching your husband doing something well and telling him that you noticed will go a long way toward affirming his spiritual growth.

If it feels as though you're on different spiritual wavelengths, don't be surprised. Be patient. Spiritual intimacy, like sexual intimacy, takes time, as the two of you grow comfortable revealing to each other the parts of your hearts that no one else sees.

Start Out Like You Can Hold Out

When we were first married, we had such ambitious plans for our spiritual life as a couple. We planned to pray together at least daily—none of those perfunctory, placid dinner-table blessings we had grown up with, mind you, but heart-focused, soul-mated prayers that would unite us around eternal things.

We planned to read to each other—devotional books, biographies of great Christians, and, of course, the Bible. And because so much of our early romance centered around music, we were sure that we would spend a lot of time singing "psalms and hymns and spiritual songs" together—Mark on the guitar, me at the piano. Our grand plans, however, failed miserably.

In the span of six months, the busyness of life and ministry kept us from even having dinner together most nights, much less having heart-to-heart prayer times. Before we went to sleep, I'd start reading to Mark, only to be interrupted by the sound of his snoring before I finished the first page. We occasionally prayed together, but our prayers were not the rich, well-prepared five-course meals we had dreamed of—more like peanut butter and jelly sandwiches grabbed on the run. And, after almost twenty-five years, I'm sure one of those leisurely times of singing together is just around the corner!

More than two decades of marriage have given me a little perspective. As newlyweds, we felt guilty for not doing enough. And at times that unnecessary guilt blocked our spiritual unity just as much as our failure did.

In our work with couples before their marriages, we encourage them with this motto with regard to spiritual things: "Start out like you can hold out." We encourage them to do so in two ways:

Pick One Just for You

Choose one spiritual practice that you will agree to do regularly *as a couple*. It doesn't matter whether it's praying together, reading a devotional book, reading the Bible at meals—we emphasize that the key is to do *something* and make it *doable*.

I was fascinated recently to read of a collection of articles by fifty-two Christian leaders on the topic of spiritual intimacy in marriage.[9] Each was asked to write a page of reflections about what they do in their own marriages to cultivate spiritual oneness. The biggest surprise was that *not one of the fifty-two couples did exactly the same thing.*

You may agree to pray at meals and to keep attending your church together. As a couple, you may decide to read a chapter out of a Christian book each week and talk about it over a Wednesday morning breakfast. Or you may choose to read a chapter from the book of Proverbs together, and invest your time in a young couples Sunday school class. The options are nearly endless.

Connect to an Imperfect Community of Faith

You will also need to have an intentional plan for connecting to a specific *imperfect* church body. We emphasize the word *imperfect,* because we've watched couples spend the early years of their marriages looking for just the "right" church. Some couples hop from church to church—a year or so at one, then on for a short time at another—unable to make a commitment to any of them.

This kind of perpetual searching sets couples up for a lifetime of dissatisfaction with their faith community and can cut them off from the transforming benefits that come only with the accountability of "doing life" with people over the long haul. Like a seed that won't embed itself in the ground in order to avoid getting dirty, couples who "just can't find" a church home miss the vital growth that happens only when we are embedded deeply into the dirty soil of God's people.

Doing these two things—marriage focused and church focused—and formulating a plan will allow you to approach the spiritual dimension of your marriage with joy and eagerness instead of guilt over somehow not doing enough. And during the dry seasons of marriage that are sure to come, your shared love for God may just hold you together when nothing else can.

4

Family of Origin: White-Water Wedding Guide

> *Let me be painfully direct here. That special person you are thinking about marrying — the one whose hand you hold under the restaurant table and who looks so irresistible in candlelight — grew up in a fallible family with imperfect parents and depraved siblings.*
>
> BILL HYBELS, *MAKING LIFE WORK*

Ah, the Ocoee River — a daring combination of class four and five rapids, the site of the kayaking venue for the 2000 Summer Olympics, and for years a favorite destination of the teenagers in our church. There's just something about the sheer unpredictability of these waters that draws visitors by the thousands to face the challenge.

Several years ago, a family from our church took their

own trip down the Ocoee. The boys were in a raft with their dad and several other men, traveling in a convoy of five or six other rafts. With explosive splashes and frantic paddling, these rubber rafts negotiated the first few rapids—with no "swimmers" reported. But after their raft had made it through the third patch of white water, they turned to wait for the rest of the boats in their group. After a few minutes of waiting, they saw a crisis unfold.

Some people were clinging to the side of an upturned raft, and there were swimmers floating downstream. Guides were shouting frantic commands to each other, and several people were jumping into the rapids with rescue equipment. With the emergency effort under way, word began to ripple upstream and downstream: A man had fallen in and was now underwater, and the teams were scrambling to pull him out before his seconds of breath ran out.

As seconds turned to minutes, and five minutes turned to fifteen, the rescue became a recovery effort, an arduous battle against the water to recover the body of the man who had drowned. As our friends waited and watched, the story became clear. The passenger had been thrown from the boat, and in an effort to get his balance, he simply did what came naturally: he put his feet down, instantly trapping them beneath a huge rock. The force of the rushing water pinned his feet so tightly that he simply couldn't dislodge himself.

Crashing currents can kill. The same currents that bring joy and pleasure bring devastation as well. It's true in white water, and it's true in marriage. What killed this man was not just the currents; it was, surprisingly, *doing what felt normal.* Over the years, he had learned that, when he felt out of control in the water, he should try to stand up. He simply did what came naturally.

How Did You Get to Be So Normal?

Over the years, we've seen couples in conflict over money or sex or in-laws, but what they're really fighting about aren't these things at all. They're really fighting about *normal*.

Every one of us enters into marriage with his or her own set of "commandments" about what is normal. But when you find yourself in explosive white water that puts you in over your head in your marriage, doing what feels normal can kill your relationship.

When Robert and Bobbie were first married, car trips for Bobbie were seen as opportunities to experience local flavor. Along the way she thought nothing of stopping at "Historical Markers" or quaint-looking shops, while Robert scratched his head in frustration as he watched his finely orchestrated, "point A to point B" itinerary disintegrate into one meandering interruption after another. It was her *normal* going head-to-head with Robert's *normal*. Bobbie's dad happily interrupted family car trips with spontaneous visits along the way. Robert's dad only stopped when the gas tank was *below* empty.

In some marriages, avoiding conflict at all costs may feel normal to the husband, while talking everything out feels normal to the wife. Then, when it comes to disagreements, they get stuck. It's not because the topic is so thorny but because they have such different ideas about the right way—the normal way—to deal with conflict.

The Unspoken Rules of Normal

Maybe it's a rule about silence at the breakfast table while the husband reads the paper. Maybe it's a rule that says "the wife always takes care of family birthdays" or "the husband always takes out the trash" or "the wife always buys the groceries." Keep your eyes open in this first year, and you'll come up with plenty of examples of your own *normals*.

Identifying your own sense of *normal* is not as easy as it may look. Most of us assume that our rules of *normal* are universal—that of course every "normal person" sees life this way. Anything else is just plain *wrong*.

When couples come to us for premarital counseling, we spend three of the five sessions focused on this critical issue of discovering each one's *normals*. For many couples, it's the first time they've ever taken a look at the assumptions hiding in the back of their minds.

There is, thankfully, a marvelous tool that can help you and your husband begin to recognize your rules of *normal* in a nonthreatening way. Couples we've worked with have consistently pointed to this tool as the single most powerful part of the premarital preparation. Here's how it works: We start with something called a genogram, which looks like a simple family tree. *Why a family tree?* you may be thinking.

Our rules of *normal* almost always come from our families of origin. Bobbie didn't just arbitrarily assume that a car trip meant stops and adventures; she learned over the course of time that this was normal for her household. On the other hand, Robert couldn't imagine it.

In all our years of premarital counseling, we've never made it a point to ask about a couple's best friends, about their favorite TV shows, or even about their most influential mentors. But we *always* ask about their families. It's not that media and friends have no impact on our values; it's just that when it comes to the imprinting of our unspoken sense of *normal*, there is no single force that comes close to the power of the family. What makes the genogram so effective is that it allows us to identify patterns of normal "in the family," not in the individual. And let's face it, most of us have a much easier time seeing the weirdness in our family than we do the weirdness in ourselves, right?

Making Your Own Genogram

To do your own genogram, you begin by each drawing a family tree that looks something like this:

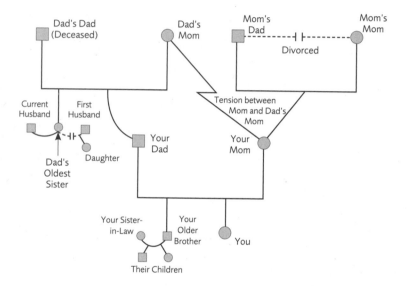

Once the drawing is done, we ask the bride or groom to give us a brief description of each person in his or her genogram. Those descriptions can vary widely from very specific comments — "president of IBM," "lifetime homemaker," or "serving time" — to more general words such as "nurturer," "strict," or "a jerk." As couples give this information, Mark urges them to say the first things that come to their minds, not to think too long about their answers. Their honest and immediate responses always provide the best clues to each one's sense of *normal*.

Once these initial descriptive notes are obtained, Mark asks for more information about parents and grandparents—always asking three questions:

- What can you tell us about their marriage?
- What can you tell us about how they dealt with conflict?
- What can you tell us about their spiritual life?

We also ask the bride and groom to identify any models of great marriages in their family systems or spots of tension between people within each of their families. From this information Mark writes a "Normal Report," which gives the bride and groom a picture of what an average person growing up in his or her family would see as normal. This report answers five questions:

1. What would someone growing up in this family system see as a normal husband?
2. What would someone growing up in this family system see as a normal wife?
3. What would someone growing up in this family system see as a normal marriage?
4. What would someone growing up in this family system see as a normal way to deal with conflict?
5. What would someone growing up in this family system see as a normal spiritual life for a married couple?

As we talk couples through the answers to these questions, the response is amazing. The vast majority of couples really get it. They leave this session with their eyes wide open, seeing their need to enter marriage prepared to do more than "what comes naturally."

Note this, too: Though there's much to be gained by working through a genogram with a trained counselor, you can experience some great success identifying *your normals* using the same process on your own.

Greg's and Carrie's Genograms

By the time Greg and Carrie finished their first premarital session, we liked them immensely. Greg seemed to be a guy who knew what he wanted out of life and marriage. He was a strong Christian with exceptionally high expectations of himself and his marriage. But during our conversation, we noticed a hint of anger just below the surface.

Carrie was a warm, responsive young woman who seemed to hang on every word that was said. By the time they arrived for the second session, they had already finished their assignments and asked if we could meet together for more than the agreed–upon five sessions!

There was nothing unusual about their genograms — showing mostly calm waters with five or six anticipated rough spots. As we talked through these, all four of us realized that there were currents beneath the surface that could present real challenges for this model young couple.

When they learned that we'd be talking about their families, Greg and Carrie laughed, describing his family as "The Cleavers" and her family as "The Simpsons." They both entered the process assuming, without question, that Greg's family was the stable one and that Carrie's was the dysfunctional one. Happily, Greg and Carrie were willing, even eager, to discover their potential danger zones.

Carrie's Family System

Carrie's parents divorced when she was a young teenager.

Her father remarried soon after the divorce. Carrie lived with her mother, whom she described as "warm, busy, insecure, and pretty lonely." Her father was "strictly business, stern, cold, and a little on the quick-tempered side," and she described her stepmother as "bossy, selfish, and manipulative."

With a hint of resentment, Carrie also explained that she had never seen her father express physical affection to either of his wives or to her. When we asked why her parents divorced, she said, "I have no idea."

"Have you ever asked either of them?" Mark inquired.

"That's just not a question you bring up with my parents," Carrie answered matter-of-factly.

Looking at Carrie's extended family, we found:

- an aunt— "nice but a little on edge all the time"—who is married to a "very successful" man who works in Europe three weeks out of every month.
- another aunt— "the loving one" — is married and divorced. Her ex-husband is a "deadbeat" who's had multiple affairs.
- a "powerhouse" uncle who is married to a "submissive" wife who has "some emotional problems."

Carrie's grandmothers are both still living; their "hardworking" and "stern" husbands both died before Carrie was born. One is a "normal grandmother" who sends cookies and birthday money. The other is described as a "witch" who "always has to have things her way."

As we completed Carrie's genogram, I asked, "Is there anything else you want to tell us about your family?"

"I'm really *so* different from them," she eagerly answered.

"I've already promised myself that I will never let the way *they* are affect my marriage."

Carrie's genogram looked something like this:

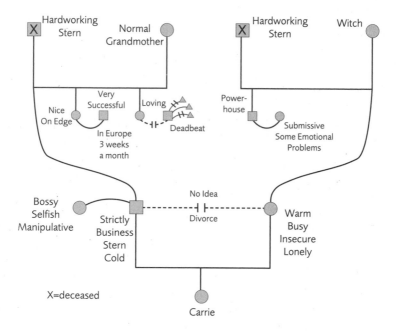

Greg's Family System

Almost every man in Greg's family is described in "larger than life" terms. Looking into his genogram, we found several interesting things:

- his father is the "undisputed boss" who "is never ever questioned."
- one of his uncles is "explosive."
- his grandfather was humorously described as "the grand pooh-bah."

- one of his uncles is "large and in charge."

He portrayed several men in his family with simple superlatives such as "amazing" or "incredible man." Many of the husbands are very spiritual men, and several are pastors.

The women in Greg's family, on the other hand, are a different story:

- a fair share of "quiet and godly" wives — but these wonderful women are described in miniature in comparison to their husbands
- an aunt with an eating disorder
- a quietly alcoholic grandmother
- Greg's mother, whose chronic back pain has kept her out of commission for the last two years
- Greg's older sister — the "black sheep" of the family
- two female cousins, each of whom have had extramarital affairs

What Lies beneath the Surface?

Did you notice that normal women in both families tended to have more than their fair share of problems? Whether it was Carrie's insecure and lonely mother or her manipulative stepmother or any of the women in Greg's family who had experienced significant emotional or physical problems, the clear rule in both systems was this: "Wives tend to have problems." Even the way the two of them introduced their families with *his* "Cleavers" versus *her* "Simpsons" stereotype gave further evidence that they were already buying into the rule — normal wives have problems.

In both families, women seemed to have a difficult time

getting their needs met in healthy ways. From affairs and addictions to vague emotional problems, it wouldn't be considered normal for a wife in this system to ask clearly for what she needs. Husbands in both systems had a pattern of being distant, out of reach, sometimes almost unapproachable. Whether they *appeared* to have it all together (like the men in Greg's system) or simply left the family (like Carrie's dad or her uncle commuting to Europe), the normal husband exhibited a pattern of not being available and of avoiding a wife's everyday struggles.

You may be wondering how this kind of pattern could be a dangerous undercurrent. Let's take an imaginary fast-forward journey five years into this marriage:

When they first got married, Greg was always the strong one, the one who had it together. Carrie loved this about Greg, and she relied on his strength. She liked him "being in charge" and taking care of her.

But now, after five years of marriage, she stares out the window, despair covering her like the blanket pulled up around her. She has her theories: Maybe it was her migraines that started a few years back, maybe it was the fact that she hasn't been able to get pregnant, maybe it was the fact that she hadn't prayed enough. But one thing seems clear to her: she no longer feels anything for this man she lives with.

He's a good man, a spiritual man. She respects him. She feels guilty that she hasn't worked hard enough to keep their marriage alive. But she's tired—tired of him never admitting he is wrong, tired of him ignoring her needs, tired of his arrogant, condescending attitude toward her whenever she brings up a problem.

How did Greg and Carrie get to this place? *They did what came naturally.* Because the men in Carrie's family are consistently distant, to keep Greg at a distance felt normal to her. Or, to overcompensate, she'd become clingy, craving Greg's attention and closeness. In Greg's case, in light of the pattern of troubled women in both families, he would blame Carrie for any unsettledness in their marriage. And Carrie might easily blame herself as well, not knowing how to ask her husband for what she really needs from him.

Carrie and Greg walked away from this genogram session with their eyes opened to the ways that the converging currents of their family systems could pose a very real threat to them. Their commitment now had a clearer focus on what it would take to keep their marriage alive and healthy. Carrie left the session with a fresh willingness to risk being attentive to *her own* needs and becoming courageous enough to share them honestly with Greg. Greg left, no longer infatuated with his own strength and convictions, but now committed to not perpetuating the pattern of placing his wife in the role of "the problem."

The Most Dangerous Enemy: The One You Don't See

It's dangerous to assume that only deeply dysfunctional people bring "issues" into their marriages. There are only two kinds of couples preparing for marriage: those who seek to be honest about the issues they bring to marriage, and those who pretend they have none. The second group is headed for the rapids unprepared.

Someone once said, "I don't know who discovered water, but I'm real sure it wasn't a fish." When we are surrounded by *normal*, it's hard for us to see that it even exists. The marriages headed for serious trouble are the ones in which one of the partners is blind to the impact of his or her patterns of *normal*. He or she says such things as —

- "My family doesn't have any effect on who I am."
- "I've known this girl for years. It won't be a problem."
- "I'm so glad we don't have any weird stuff in our families."

Five years into our marriage, Mark and I entered some white water without being ready. Mark was sent for three days of psychological testing by a future employer. Looking back now, almost twenty years later, we laugh about this—the kind of nervous laughter that happens after you've just barely avoided an accident. But when we first heard the assessment, we weren't laughing.

After Mark completed his three days of testing, we sat in the vocational therapist's office waiting to hear the results. Anticipating a predictable outcome, we were actually looking forward to this report. Mark always performed well on tests, and we expected to hear such words as *highly motivated, exceptional,* and *wise beyond his years.* What we heard, however, was very different.

Turning toward me, the counselor said, "I want you to know that your husband is a very angry man." I stared in disbelief. Mark laughed. He really did. In fact, Mark was sure that the counselor had mixed up his report with someone else's. I'll never forget the way my husband looked at me—the woman he had lived with for five years. He said, "Tell him, honey. Am I an angry man? I'm the funny guy, remember? There may be other angry men in my family, but I'm not one of them."

But to Mark's amazement, I could not disagree with the counselor. In fact, I corroborated his report with supplemental evidence of my own. If you had asked Mark at that time,

"How does your family affect your marriage?" he would have been resolute: "Not very much. Our marriage is nothing like my parents' marriage." What Mark couldn't see was that his family *had* deeply influenced him. He was blind to the obvious. He was about to step into the same profession as the majority of men in his family and had already begun to live with some of the same unacknowledged patterns of anger. It was just *normal*.

During the subsequent months and years, Mark began the process of openly acknowledging his anger, eventually learning that if he didn't own it, it would own him and hold our family hostage. Once he recognized the dangerous undercurrent of anger, Mark was free to be playful about it.

When we lead marriage retreats, Mark loves to tell a story about how my playfulness has, at times, helped to free him from his anger. For reasons that will be obvious, I'll let Mark tell the story in his own words:

> Ten years into our marriage, I came home to a house that looked like three wild children lived there (they did, of course). Toys were strewn all over the playroom. Dishes were unwashed. There was a half-made sandwich on the counter that had obviously been there for hours.
>
> I'd had a particularly difficult day at work. I felt the anger rising in me. I quickly forgot the niceties. There was no "How was your day?" or "How can I help with dinner?" I simply came into the house, set my jaw, and began cleaning — "immaculating," as my children now call it. And before long, I had convinced myself of the absolute injustice of having to come home and clean a messy house after working long hours all day long.

But my bride, who knows my genogram way too well, has learned how to interrupt my petty patterns of anger. I'll never forget that intense moment in the kitchen. After observing me huffing around for a few minutes, she resisted the urge to hook into my anger. She could have easily reacted by explaining that this just happened to be the maid's decade off, or she might have shot back with "I'm sorry you didn't marry June Cleaver."

Instead, she said, "Here's what I want you to do: I want you to take off your tie, lie down on our bed for a few minutes, open that book you've been wanting to read, and then call me in a few minutes. When I get there, I want you to tell me how much you love me. Then maybe we can start all over again."

What Are We Arguing about Anyway?

In the heat of conflict, it's easy to become confused about what the real issues are. Our experience has been this: the more a couple focuses on the content of the conflict—issues like money, sex, in-laws, a messy kitchen—the more likely it is that they'll remain stuck in the conflict. On the other hand, the more a couple focuses on their genogram issues—patterns of anger and reaction, dominance and subservience, or power and helplessness—the more likely they'll move through those issues with love and respect intact.

The mistake most couples make when working through conflict is to focus on the wrong issue. For example, the domineering husband and the submissive wife may have a conflict about sex, but sex isn't the real issue. Or there may be a nagging wife and an unresponsive husband who think their conflict is about the children, but the real issue is the nagging/ unresponsiveness pattern.

Jim and Irene weren't so fortunate. As we met with them week after week, they couldn't get beyond the assumption that their only real problem was money. One night, within earshot of their children, they were arguing about money yet again. The conflict escalated out of control, and Jim slapped Irene so hard that he broke her nose. They stood in startled amazement over what he had done. Blood began to run down Irene's face as their eight-year-old son ran into the room with his piggy bank, shouting, "You can have all of my money!"

Like the child who thinks the piggy bank will help, we can miss seeing the most dangerous currents of *normal* beneath our disagreements. It's these currents, not the subject matter of these disagreements, that will pose the greatest threat to your marriage.

5

Roles: Welcome to My World

A major source of love for a man is the loving reaction that a woman has to his behavior. He has a love tank, too, but his is not necessarily filled by what she does for him. Instead, it is mainly filled by how she reacts to him or how she feels about him. A man's heart opens as he succeeds in fulfilling a woman.

JOHN GRAY, MEN ARE FROM MARS. WOMEN ARE FROM VENUS

———◆•◆×◆•◆———

Back in 1955, in a magazine called *Housekeeping Monthly,* an article for women appeared in the May 13 edition. It was titled "The Good Wife's Guide,"[10] and it outlined, in detail, the unique role a wife should play in a healthy marriage. In that very different world, expectations for wives were so clearly prescribed that they appear laughable to us today.

Here are a few of those tips for being a "good wife"—at least in the 1950s:

- Have dinner ready. Plan ahead, even the night before, to have a delicious meal ready, on time for his return. This is a way of letting him know that you have been thinking about him and are concerned about his needs.

- Prepare yourself. Take fifteen minutes to rest so you'll be refreshed when he arrives. Touch up your makeup, put a ribbon in your hair, and be fresh looking.

- Be a little gay and a little more interesting for him. His boring day may need a lift and one of your duties is to provide it.

- Clear away the clutter. Take one last trip through the main part of the house just before your husband arrives. Gather up schoolbooks, toys, paper, etc., and then run a dust cloth over the tables.

- During the cooler months of the year you should prepare and light a fire for him to unwind by. Your husband will feel he has reached a haven of rest and order, and it will give you a lift, too. After all, catering for his comfort will provide you with immense personal satisfaction.

- Prepare the children. Take a few minutes to wash the children's hands and faces (if they are small), comb their hair, and, if necessary, change their clothes. They are little treasures, and he would like to see them playing the part. Minimize all noise. At the time of his arrival, eliminate all noise of the washer, dryer, or vacuum cleaner. Try to encourage the children to be quiet.

- Greet him with a warm smile and show sincerity in your desire to please him.

- Listen to him. You may have a dozen important things to tell him, but the moment of his arrival is not the time. Let him talk first—remember, his topics of conversation are more important than yours.
- Make the evening his. Never complain if he comes home late or goes out to dinner or to other places of entertainment without you. Instead, try to understand his world of strain and pressure and his very real need to be at home and relax.
- Don't complain if he's home late for dinner or even if he stays out all night. Count this as minor compared to what he might have gone through that day.
- Make him comfortable. Have him lean back in a comfortable chair or have him lie down in the bedroom. Have a cool or warm drink ready for him. Arrange his pillow and offer to take off his shoes. Speak in a low, soothing, and pleasant voice.
- Don't ask him questions about his actions or question his judgment or integrity. Remember, he is the master of the house and as such will always exercise his will with fairness and truthfulness. You have no right to question him.

I'm sure you can imagine the responses we get when we read this prescription to couples. With each line of advice, the laughter only gets louder.

Back in the 1950s, the wife's role was prescribed with rigid clarity. And though this well-defined role was not exactly a recipe for exceptional marriages, there is little doubt that such clarity served at times to make marriages more stable, if less passionate. A man knew his role; a woman knew hers. And though a transformation of these expectations, particularly for wives, was undeniably necessary, the move toward more "egalitarian" marriages has frequently resulted in *less* equality and more rancorous confusion, not unlike a baseball team that plays with the vague idea that everyone should play every position. Balls get dropped, bases are left uncovered, accusations fly, and, more often than not, the team loses.

I was fascinated recently to read about the surprising results of a study of college students at three universities (Brandeis, UCLA, and Whittier College). Here's what the study revealed: "College-age couples who hold traditional views about gender roles are much more likely to make enduring marriages than couples who subscribe to egalitarian precepts."[11] There seems to be something about knowing our positions on the playing field of marriage that brings a protective stability to relationships between husbands and wives.

Whenever I teach about the Bible's perspective on the role of the wife in a marriage, I can feel the level of defensiveness rising before I even begin to speak. Actually, the defensiveness comes quite naturally. Many women have become appropriately angered by the self-serving spirituality of men who assume that their biblical role as husbands gives them the right to dominate and control their wives. But the Bible's message about our roles in marriage is quite different.

At first glance, when we look to the Bible for teaching about specific roles for husbands and wives, what we find seems disappointingly vague. Who pays the bills, who plans the vacation, who cleans the house, who shops for groceries, who has a career, who changes the diapers—none of these are answered in Scripture with regard to gender. But the Bible does something much more profound than prescribing specific tasks for husbands and other tasks for wives. When understood clearly, the roles the Bible describes for wives in marriage can free us from the tired oppositional approach to gender roles that easily results from assuming that men and women are from different planets.

So if a vague egalitarian approach does not work and the traditional model of the 1950s is distasteful at best (oppressive at worst), it may be time to consider a radically different option. The Bible, while not prescribing specific tasks, does give at least three clear directives for women about their role in marriage—describing attitudes that Christian wives are called to take toward their husbands. As you consider what the Bible has to say about roles in marriage, remember that *you* are in the driver's seat. Your husband cannot force you to adopt these attitudes. And, in fact, these attitudes *only* work when they're freely chosen by you.

Image Conscious

> So God created man in his own image,
>   in the image of God he created him;
>   male and female he created them.
>
> GENESIS 1:27

Even a quick reading of the creation story in Genesis 1 and 2 shows a God who fashions with order and purpose. Each stage of the creation builds, each is more complex, each is better than the one before—until the creation climaxes to its peak. And what, exactly, was this pinnacle?

I've heard Bible teachers explain that creation reached its highest point when God breathed life into Adam. But as I've read the story more closely, this interpretation seems implausible to me. After each stage of creation, we hear the rhythmic refrain, "And God saw that it was good." But after the creation of Adam, after Adam was placed in the garden, instead of hearing the consistent cadence of "it was good," the rhythm of creation is interrupted with four shocking words, "It is *not* good."[12] *What?* you may be thinking. *How can what God has created be somehow* not *good?* "It is not good," God says, "for the man to be alone." Apart from the creation of the woman, the creation story is simply incomplete. The man by himself is not enough.

And like a fireworks display that teases the crowd with a dramatic pause just before the grand finale—waiting long enough that the crowd begins to assume the show is over—God saves his best for last. Scripture does not teach, as some would have us believe, that the woman is an afterthought, a garnish on the real deal of creation, an inferior appendage to the main attraction. If we pay close attention to the story, it's hard to miss the fact that in this narrative the woman is nothing less than the pinnacle of God's creation, a unique portrait of the image of God.

While Adam was sleeping, God didn't make a secretary, a concierge, a pet, or a maid for him. God made someone who would answer Adam's aching aloneness, one so totally *united* to Adam that they would enjoy an exclusive oneness together.

In revealing the image of God, your husband and you each are part of the dance. God is best revealed not in some sort of neutered, unisex, genderless creation but in a gender-full creation—a creation in which husbands and wives are free to be fully man and fully woman.

Scripture invites us to see God uniquely displayed in our maleness and femaleness—in the passionate partnership between a husband and a wife. In marriage we have a picture of the rock-solid dependability and strength of God, in fluid partnership with the beauty and desirability of God, our unveiled Treasure who is to be worshiped and pursued. Psalm 62 hints at this gender-full nature of God:

One thing God has spoken,
  two things have I heard:
that you, O God, are strong,
  and that you, O Lord, are loving.

PSALM 62:11–12

We can laugh about and be challenged by the startling differences between men and women. Yet, according to Scripture, these differences are no accident. They are, in fact, the intentional gift of a good God.[13]

Mark officiated at a wedding not long ago in which he made some personal remarks to the bride and the groom. As he spoke to the bride, he said, "Jenny, you are God's gift to Michael." Jenny laughed loudly. Even in the nervousness of the moment, it caught her by surprise that she could be called "God's gift" to anyone.

A woman who doesn't know who she is will settle for much less than God's best in her marriage. She is God's gift to her husband—God's image bearer. Without this knowledge, she will come to believe that she is not worth fighting for. She will come to assume that any unacceptable treatment she receives from her husband is only what she deserves. She will give up on her grand dreams of loving a man who delights in her.

Help Me!

> But for Adam no suitable helper was found. So the LORD God caused the man to fall into a deep sleep; and while he was sleeping, he took one of the man's ribs and closed up the place with flesh. Then the LORD God made a woman from the rib he had taken out of the man, and he brought her to the man.
>
> GENESIS 2:20b–22

Eve is formed as the suitable *helper* of Adam. I have to admit that, when I first read this word in the creation story, it seemed as though Eve had been given some sort of second-class status, as though the real action remained with Adam. Eve, beautiful though she might have been, appeared somewhere in the background, perhaps cooking for and cleaning up after the real star of the show.

But as I've studied this story over the years, a very different picture has come into focus. I was fascinated to discover that, apart from its use in this story to describe Eve, this specific word for *help* is used in Scripture almost always to describe God (not exactly a bit role in the universe, eh?). After the birth of Cain, Eve said, "With the *help* of the LORD I have brought forth a man."[14] Israel's King David later cried out, "Do not hide your face from me, do not turn your servant away in anger; you have been my *helper*."[15]

And in the book of Deuteronomy, we get an even clearer picture of what this help looks like:

> There is no one like the God of Jeshurun,
>   who rides on the heavens to *help* you
>   and on the clouds in his majesty.
> The eternal God is your refuge,
>   and underneath are the everlasting arms.
> He will drive out your enemy before you.
>   DEUTERONOMY 33:26–27, emphasis added

In the Gospel of John in the New Testament, the Holy Spirit is referred to by the Greek word sometimes translated Helper.[16] The condescension ("Look, it's Daddy's little helper!") we sometimes associate with the word is completely absent. Instead *helper* paints a picture of one who comes to rescue just in the nick of time.

Back in 1990, Bobbie played that very role in Robert's life. For six years, he and Bobbie had struggled to keep alive the entrepreneurial venture that was a dream come true just a few years earlier. But that February Robert received a devastating phone call from his banker telling him that the note was being called on his business. Suddenly they were faced with the reality of closing their office and sending sixteen employees home with no paycheck and an uncertain future. Because they had pledged their home for the bank loan, their personal equity was gone. Robert's confidence was understandably shaken.

The next day, with countless details to manage, Bobbie sprang into action. Like a warrior, she used the only weapons at her disposal—her time, her compassion, and her words. After each employee was told there would be no more work, Bobbie hugged them and cried with them. As the office furniture was loaded into a van, Robert and Bobbie stood together in shocked silence. Then, sitting on the carpeted floor of a once beautiful executive office, with only a phone left in the room, Bobbie began calling clients. As she dialed each number, she prayed for the person who would be receiving the message that their business had been forced to close. After each conversation, she calmly reported to Robert. With confidence and tenderness she continued the recovery operation until every client and merchant had been contacted.

When a husband's back is against the wall, the wife is like the cavalry that charges over the hill. The wife is like Superman or the Lone Ranger, stepping in to save the one who cannot rescue himself. The wife is the one who is strong enough to believe in her husband when he may be too weak to believe in himself. In fact, in those few instances in the Bible when *helper* is not used to refer to God, it always refers to a warrior who rescues others in a battle.

Embracing our role as helpers doesn't prevent us, though, from having a life of our own. Just take a look at how the biblical version of the ideal wife—"the Proverbs 31 woman"—spends her time:

- She runs an import/export business (31:13–14).
- She manages employees (31:15).
- She buys real estate (31:16).
- She receives a financial gain on her investments (31:16).
- She plants a vineyard (31:16).
- She earns a profit from her business (31:18).
- She gives to the poor and needy (31:20).
- She furnishes her house (31:22).
- She dresses well (31:22).
- She is a wholesaler of products to other merchants (31:24).
- She teaches (31:26).
- She runs a household (31:27).
- Her success earns her public praise (31:31).

All of this is accomplished because she takes the initiative. Ironically, behind every Proverbs 31 woman is a Proverbs 31 husband—a man secure enough in his own strength that he isn't threatened by the successes of his bride.

Your husband needs you as a helper. He may not know it; he may not admit it. But he needs you.

Is Submission Really a Dirty Word?

Submit to one another out of reverence for Christ. Wives, submit to your husbands as to the Lord. . . . Husbands, love your wives, just as Christ loved the church and gave himself up for her. . . .

However, each one of you also must love his wife as he loves himself, and the wife must respect her husband.

Ephesians 5:21–22, 25, 33

When I told Mark that Bobbie and I were going to address submission in this chapter, his eyebrows rose and he got that playful little smirk he gets whenever he thinks I've bitten off more than I can chew. We've both seen how easily this topic can spark controversy. We've seen fire in the eyes of people in our Sunday school classes when we even mention the word. We've watched defenses fly up faster than a force field on the Starship Enterprise.

We are convinced that a biblical understanding of submission holds a key to our experiencing marriage at its best. But in order to use this key, we have to first understand clearly what Scripture means when it urges a wife to submit to her husband. Though there is more than enough room for clouds of confusion on this topic, we can be clear that submission in the Bible means at least two things:

Submission Is Mutual

In Ephesians 5, the primary role of husbands and wives in marriage is defined: "Submit to one another." Here, submission is not related to gender at all. In the apostle Paul's male-dominated culture, the notion of husbands *ever* submitting to their wives undoubtedly sounded scandalous. But Paul was on to something. The truth is that healthy adults all submit to something—whether it is to the truth, to love, to God, to a relationship, or to the board of directors.

No relationship, in fact, can succeed without submission. And in reality, in the healthiest marriages we've ever seen, there is a sort of reverse tug-of-war in which husband and wife make a game of who can give victory to the other partner first.

Submission Is Voluntary

Paul never advises husbands to *make* their wives submit. In fact, the command to husbands is just the opposite. Instead of telling husbands, "Make your wives behave," Paul advises them simply to "love your wives" as radically and sacrificially "as Christ loved the church." Christian husbands who lay the "submission trip" on their wives are missing the point entirely, since the only way that submission can work *for* the marriage is when it is given voluntarily and without compulsion.

The biblical model of submission is this: the willing choice of a wife to submit freely to her husband and his willingness to lovingly submit to her. Watch people who have healthy marriages, and you'll see this kind of willful submission happening all the time:

- the wife who accepts with grace her husband's recommended cuts to the family budget; the husband who accepts the same from his wife
- the husband who moves to a new town because of an unparalleled career opportunity offered to his wife; the wife who moves for the sake of her husband's career change
- the wife who occasionally chooses to watch the game with her husband, giving up a cozy chair and a gripping novel; the husband who attends a concert with his wife when she's bought special tickets
- the husband who goes to the romantic comedy instead of the action adventure movie; the wife who willingly goes to his choice of a show

- the wife who fills the car with gas instead of waiting for him to do it; the husband who stops to fill the car's gas tank for his wife

Mark and I have an understanding that goes something like this: "If we ever get stuck and we're unable to agree on what to do, I want you to win." It is in and through this voluntary kind of yielding that the marriage always wins.

What Submission Is *Not*

After agreeing together on what submission is, it's important that we be clear about at least a couple of things that submission is not:

Submission Does Not Turn a Wife into a Passive Pawn

Biblical submission is not about a woman giving up on her passions, her dreams, her opinions, or her identity in order to please her husband. If your husband wants to move across the country to take on a new job opportunity and you feel uneasy about it, tell him. Openly express your reservations. Tell him exactly how you feel and why. Responding with a "whatever you want, honey" passivity and pretending to be in total agreement are not accurate expressions of submission. They're *dishonest* expressions.

Several years ago, Mark and I were at a stalemate on a decision. We were behind on several bills. They were "forgiving bills," not like credit cards that charge interest; they were bills to the doctor, debt payments to family members—that kind of thing. Normally, I handle the bills in our house, but one day Mark decided that we needed to go ahead and pay these bills, even if it meant dipping into our savings. I wasn't convinced of the wisdom of that decision. I pointed out that we were anticipating receiving some additional money in the next couple months. I reminded him of how much we hate to live so close to the edge. I urged him to wait to pay the bills. But after making my case, here was my concluding thought: "But I trust you. And I will support whatever you decide on this one."

We went ahead and paid the bills. Was it the right thing to do? Maybe. Did I yield to Mark's influence because he is "the man of the house"? No. There have, in fact, been many times when he responded in the same way for me—courageously and sacrificially ending a difference of opinion before it became an argument. But in this case, I simply trusted him to make the final call. Either way, we invite each other into maturity and love.

Submission Does Not Require a Wife to Tolerate Abuse

You may be saying, "Okay, a mutual and voluntary kind of submission makes sense, but what about a wife in an abusive marriage? Does the Bible teach that she should submit to her husband if he abuses her, destroying her with caustic words or with violent hands?"

These are the very questions Jean asked me a few years ago as we ate lunch together. She and Frank had been married for less than six months, and she had just moved out of her newlywed apartment. I swallowed hard, bit my tongue, and listened.

Pulling up her sleeve, Jean showed me month-old bruises, and asked if I supported her decision to move out.

My eyes welled up with tears as I looked into Jean's face. "Love," I said, "does not require you to be a willing partner in your husband's destructive behavior. You've done the right thing. Now you must confront him clearly and firmly with a message that says unequivocally, *I love you, but this is not acceptable.*" I said, "Unless he's willing to change immediately, the most loving thing you can do is to separate." I gave her the names of several Christian doctors and organizations in our area that specialized in abuse counseling.[17]

If you or someone you know is dealing with a husband's physical, verbal, or emotional abuse, alcoholism, philandering, or pornography—or any form of violent behavior—please get help. You have no obligation to give in to this. This is *not* submission. In fact, love *requires* your protection of yourself and the vows you made.

Dancing the Roles

In our bathroom we have a picture of dancers in each others' arms. It's a Renoir painting called "A Dance in the Country." A bearded young man is holding his beaming partner in his arms. I get the impression that he has just whispered something into her ear—something she finds exceedingly charming or funny.

Over the years, as Mark and I have talked about the peculiar roles that each of us play in our marriage, we've found no better picture than our "Dance in the Country." We can't dance well together without a willingness to be mutually responsive to each other. We'll never enjoy the music as long as we're rigidly focused on the inflexible "rules" of the dance. The waltz will always work best if our steps are fluid and graceful—sometimes he moves forward and I follow, and sometimes I set the pace.

Great marriages *are* great dances, and those who are willing to move together nimbly will have the most fun of all.

6

Talk: Did Someone Hit the Mute Button?

*So you look at us with one of those 250,000
facial expressions you can make as a woman,
put your hand on your hip, and say things like,
"When are you going to get with the program!"
Many men do not have a clue to the program!*

GARY SMALLEY, *THE HIDDEN VALUE OF A MAN*

At their first premarital counseling session, Charlie and Meredith couldn't keep their hands off each other. They moved their chairs as close together as they could get them. They talked about how much they loved being together, how conversation flowed so naturally, how comfortable they felt with each other. Mark and I found this kind of open affection refreshing.

We got around to the topic of communication in marriage. As we began to talk about some challenges they were likely to face, they looked at us in disbelief, with expressions you might expect to see on the face of Michael Jordan receiving ball-handling tips from my mother. These lovebirds made it clear that this was information for some other couple, not for them.

"We appreciate your concern for us," they politely interrupted, "but we've got to tell you, this is an area where we just don't need any help."

At this point, I couldn't help thinking of Yoda's promise to Luke. I remembered young Skywalker in his training, saying, "But Master Yoda, I'm not scared." Yoda's head rolled slowly to one side as he responded, with eyes locked on his young apprentice, "You will be. You *will* be."

The vast majority of couples we've counseled have had very little difficulty with conversation — before the wedding, that is. During the premarital "falling in love" stage, conversation can feel a lot like jumping off a diving board. After the leap, there's plenty of gravity to keep you moving in the right direction, and very little effort is required to get you where you need to go. During this stage, couples typically find themselves talking with comfort and ease. But after the wedding, it can feel a lot more like swimming in the deep end. You only stay afloat with effort.

One woman may enter marriage with an unquestioning "he completes me" attitude. But within the first year, that same woman can find herself in postmarital shock, as simple conversation becomes increasingly difficult with the man who used to be her soul mate. And when Captain Understanding mutates into Dr. Clueless, a bride can naturally feel as though someone changed all the rules without telling her.

There are few areas where the differences between men and women are more obvious than in the area of conversation. And though not every man fits into every stereotypical description, there are certain qualities about many men and their communication styles that, if you learn them in this first year, can save you years of frustration.

Is Deafness Really a Part of His Gender Coding?

We don't have to look far to find complaints and jokes about husbands who just don't seem to listen. C. S. Lewis put these words in the mouth of one of his fictional characters: "Husbands were made to be talked to. It helps them concentrate their minds on what they're reading."[18] More recently, a Christian nonfiction writer wrote these clearly *nonfictional* words: "Husbands, listen to your wives. Wives, speak the truth in love to your deaf husbands."[19] And even Jane Austen, in her book *Sense and Sensibility*, affirms, "Between lovers, no subject, no communication is even made till it has been made at least twenty times over."[20]

I hope you understand. Husbands have a God-given mandate to cherish their wives, to listen to them, to respond to their needs. And most of them enter marriage with the absolute intention of doing just that. So why do these well-intentioned husbands often fail when it comes to really communicating with their wives?

Imagine this scene: Your husband is lost. Against his nature as it is, he finally breaks down and decides to ask for directions. (I know this isn't a fiction book, but stay with me.) He sees a man walking a dog in a residential neighborhood, pulls over, rolls down the window, and asks, "Excuse me, could you tell me how to get downtown?" But instead of answering, the guy keeps walking.

Your husband gives the guy the benefit of the doubt and assumes the pedestrian just didn't hear him. So he pulls forward and speaks again—this time more loudly: "Hey, mister, I'm lost! You want to give me some directions?" This time the man just stares, opens his mouth to say something, then shrugs his shoulders a little, and keeps walking. By this time, your boy is not happy.

Finally, he steps out of the car, approaches to within a few feet from the stranger, and asks for directions a third time. The stranger can see the frustration and anger all over your husband's face, and words immediately begin to fly from the stranger's mouth. But your husband can't understand a thing the guy is saying. Why not? *He's speaking in Chinese.*[21]

Once we realize that the object of our frustration doesn't have a clue what we are saying, anger no longer makes sense, does it? But husbands and wives often find themselves trapped in patterns of anger created by a very similar problem. It's as though we are speaking completely different languages. Call it "Mars and Venus"; call it "his needs and her needs"; call it different "love languages." But there does seem to be general agreement that men and women communicate in very different ways. Because you and your husband both use the same vocabulary and the same grammar, you can easily assume that, when you send a message—which you understand—to your husband, he will understand the message that was sent—exactly as you understood it.

Misunderstandings in conversations between husbands and wives do not only occur around situations of intense conflict. They happen all the time, particularly to couples who have never recognized their tendency to speak different languages. Consider this hypothetical conversation:

> *Wife:* "You never hold me anymore. You could tell how sad I was this morning after I heard the news about my mom. I needed you to hug me, but you just avoided me."

Husband: "I thought you needed some space. How was I supposed to know you needed a hug? If you needed a hug, why didn't you just ask me?"

Wife: "That's exactly the point. I shouldn't *have* to ask you. You know how much I need affection. Before we got married, you sure didn't have trouble showing me affection. Now it's like I have to turn in a request form just to get you to hold my hand."

Husband: "You're doing it again. If I don't hug you, I get in trouble. If I offer to hug you, I still get in trouble. No matter what I do, you're not satisfied."[22]

Something got lost in the translation, didn't it? What this wife is saying is that she loves to be close to her husband and would be thrilled if he'd take the initiative to hold her more often, especially when she's going through tough times. What her husband hears is that he's in trouble for not being able to read his wife's mind. You see, when you bring a concern to your husband, he'll typically assume one of two things: (1) that you want him to fix the problem (resulting in advice giving), or (2) that he's being attacked (resulting in defensiveness). These assumptions are his default settings.

Let's face it. Something in us really does want our husbands to read our minds. I would love it if Mark always knew exactly what to do for me without my having to say a word. But he needs me to tell him!

What the husband in this dialogue is trying to say is that he loves his wife and is willing to hold her or to give her space or to do whatever else she needs, but that he doesn't always know what she wants from him. He is saying that he needs more clarity from her. What she hears, though, is that he doesn't love her the way he used to love her.

Deafness is *not* an inherent part of your husband's genetic coding. He is simply wired to hear things differently from what you intended to communicate. But language differences need not push you apart. If you've ever had a dinner guest whose command of the English language is limited, you know what I mean. We've shared dinners with people whose knowledge of English is equivalent to our knowledge of their language. At first, conversation is difficult, but by the end of the evening, we are leaning in toward each other, intensely listening in order to understand, often laughing at ourselves as we play impromptu charades.

Differences in the way you communicate with your husband can either launch you into a cold war of misunderstanding or draw you closer, leaving you loving and laughing with each other as you lean in to gain greater levels of understanding.

Relational Amnesia

What happened? Tori wondered, nine months into her marriage. During the three years she dated Wes, they talked effortlessly for hours on end. But now it seemed to be so much work.

Finally she asked her husband, "What happened? I know we know how to do this!"

Wes was more right than he realized when he joked, "Maybe we just forgot."

It happens to most couples. We spend months, even years, in a courtship filled with incredible conversations. But a few months or years into the marriage, it's easy to develop what we call "relational amnesia." Forgetting the ways we used to talk, we settle into patterns of conversation that are unsatisfactory to both of us. When it happens to you, two principles can help you overcome this amnesia:

- *Remember* the little things you said and did when your relationship was new and growing.
- *Repeat* those words and patterns by intentionally saying and doing what came so naturally during your courtship.

Almost without exception, what we are looking for in conversations with our husbands is to *know their hearts*. For many of us, it was the fact that our husbands allowed us glimpses into their hearts and told us things they had never told anyone else that gave us such certainty that "this is the one."

It may not be an overstatement to say that a wife longs to know her husband's soul with the same intensity that a husband longs to know his wife's body. And just as there are certain things your husband can do that are huge sexual turnoffs to you, the words you speak can either swing open or slam shut your husband's spirit.

Can Openers to Your Husband's Soul

To help you open the door to your groom's heart, we've developed what we call "Can Openers to Your Husband's Soul."

Can Opener #1: Conversational Clarity

In the dialogue on pages 69–70, the husband and wife both wound up frustrated—unable to communicate what they were really trying to say. Of course, in the wife's mind, it was absolutely clear what the husband should have done. He should have "figured it out" and just held her when she heard the news about her mom.

Though you may naturally expect your husband to understand what you need without obvious communication from you, my advice is, *Don't count on it!* A woman who waits around for her husband to figure out what it is that she needs from him will likely be waiting a very long time.

Early in our marriage, Mark learned that I didn't want to "be fixed" when I went to him with a problem. Sometimes I simply needed him to listen. And so he learned to listen and seldom offered his opinion. But we discovered—the hard way—that Mark's listening-only response wasn't always what I really wanted. Sometimes I *did* want Mark to come up with a few ideas, and still other times I really did want him to make a decision. But, Murphy's Law being what it is, Mark almost always guessed wrong—he advised when he should have listened; he listened when I really wanted his input; he gave options when I really just needed a decision.

Recognizing that I don't always need the same kind of response from him every time, one day Mark tried out a solution to our "translation frustration." He said something like this: "Is this one of those times when you want my advice, or do you need me to make a decision, or do you just want me to listen?" His question helped me clarify for myself what I needed from him.

Take a typical conversation about where I wanted to go for dinner:

> *Mark:* "Where would you like to go out for dinner this weekend?"
>
> *Me:* "I don't know. Where do you want to go?"

Now, remember—at this point, Mark is simply wanting to make me happy, to take me to a place I would enjoy. He really doesn't care where we go to dinner. But he's in a quandary as to how to respond. He could say, "I don't care," but I might be tired of making decisions and just want him to pick a place. He could simply choose a restaurant, but he really wants to go somewhere that I will enjoy. He could give me a list of options. He could plan the whole date on his own and completely surprise me. So now Mark has learned that, before he responds to this very simple question, he needs help with the translation.

> *Mark:* "Babe, is this one of those times when you want me just to plan the whole date so you don't have to worry about it, or is it one of those times you've got a special place in mind where you'd really like to go, or is this one of those times when you want me to give you a list of options and let you pick the place you'd like to go?"
>
> *Me:* "Actually, this is one of those times when . . ."

As simple—or absurd—as it may sound, these seven words ("this is one of those times when . . .") can do wonders for the translation frustration and lead to open and productive conversation with your husband.

Many men stop being conversationalists with their wives because too many conversations end with the husband feeling as though he just didn't get it right. As a result he begins to say such things as "I'm just not good at mind reading" or "communication is just not my thing."

Mark plays golf the same way a lot of men communicate. Early in his golfing career, he decided—with the help of a few overly honest friends—that he stunk at the game. Once he made that decision—after just five games—guess how often he played. Though he is surrounded by good friends who love to play golf, he hasn't picked up a club in ten years.

When a man becomes convinced that he is "no good at talking" with his wife, he stops playing the conversation game altogether. Practicing the "Can Opener of Conversational Clarity" can help your husband feel like a success and can go a long way toward keeping him in the game.

Can Opener #2: Third-Object Conversation

Think about how men typically build friendships: by *doing something*—on the athletic field, around a poker table, in a foxhole, in front of a television, on a mission trip. Women, on the other hand, are quite content to build friendships just by talking. Take a stroll through a coffee shop and you'll see what I mean. Two women sitting together—nothing but coffee and conversation between them. But two men will usually have something there—their newspapers, their Day-Timers, their Palm Pilots, sometimes just a napkin on which they are graphing their ideas. When men talk, there is almost always a third object.

Mark has a close friend who is a pastor. They meet together at least once a week for an hour and a half or so. They have incredible conversations about family, work, fears, and failures. They pray together and challenge each other, and they also have comfortable times of silence. And they do all of this *while they're running.*

Here's what you can learn: Talking with each other during a shared activity can be the doorway for your husband to begin to tell you what really matters to him. Because good conversation is important to you, make it your job to find opportunities for third-object conversations. For example, when he's headed out the door on Saturday morning to go to his favorite home improvement store, offer to go along. Your conversation in the car and as you wander the aisles will come naturally.

While she was in her seventies, Bobbie's mother-in-law found a way to create conversations with her often quiet husband by leasing a small garden plot. Twice a week they rode their bikes from their condominium to their tiny vegetable farm. And for her, the results were more wonderful than basketfuls of plump tomatoes or fresh green snap peas.

You and I often get to substantive conversation through non-directed — what our husbands might consider "pointless" — conversation. Let me explain what I mean. Your husband might think, *Why would my wife care about the boring details of my day? She's just being kind by asking, so I'll do her the favor of not wasting her time with a lot of useless trivia.*

And so when you ask about his day, he gives you the "Cliffs Notes" version, which usually lasts no more than fifteen seconds. You feel hurt, wondering why he doesn't want to share his life with you. Your husband thinks he's being kind by not boring you with the details. But he must learn that meandering conversation — sharing what he may see as pointless detail — is the most direct route to opening your heart to him.

Can Opener #3: Pillow Talk

The application of this third can opener — pillow talk — takes place in a specific place and at a specific time, namely, in your bedroom in the few moments you have together just before you go to sleep at night.

Mark is a morning person, and I'm a night owl, but we're together on this idea. Pillow talk doesn't require the same schedule every night, but it does require that, at least once a week, you both make a point of heading to bed at the same time.

First, let me be clear about what you don't want to talk about during pillow talk. It's not the time to bring up potentially contentious topics or ones that require the expenditure of a good deal of energy. As a matter of fact, as a general rule we recommend that couples avoid difficult topics after 7:00 P.M. I've never seen any studies on this, but I'm sure most couples have their worst conflicts late in the evenings when they are exhausted and easily frustrated. So be careful not to push your husband to resolve a conflict when both of you are potentially at your worst. On those occasions when you must deal with a specific source of frustration, do it with both feet on the floor, eyeball to eyeball.

Pillow talk is also *not* the time for the kind of romantic exchange that demands a response. This is a for-free gift that you give your husband, not expecting anything in return. You can ruin perfect pillow talk by saying, "I love you so much," then pausing to wait for a response and going on to say, "Well—don't you have anything to say?!" That's *not* a for-free gift.

Pillow talk is, however, a way to seal the end of your day with kind, flirtatious, and encouraging words that remind your husband of your love for him. Your husband can even fall asleep while you're in the middle of pillow talk. That's okay. What you are doing is creating a context for conversation with your husband that is pleasantly intimate because he *cannot fail.*

During pillow talk, he can enjoy listening without worrying that he may say something stupid. As your husband ends his day hearing such things as, "Have I told you lately how much I love you?" or "I loved it when you called me in the middle of your day today," he will see conversation with you as a safe and delightful place to be. This is the time for unqualified encouraging words. So be careful not to ruin perfectly good pillow talk by taking a statement such as "You are so compassionate to strangers" and then adding, "Why don't you ever treat me that well?"

Here's the important principle: When you want to get close to your husband, you only set yourself up for frustration by expecting him to do the talking. Comments like "You never talk to me" only push him away. But when you take the initiative to offer "for-free" conversation—a safe place where he cannot fail—he is much more likely to feel close to you and be willing to risk talking more in the future.

Your husband's heart can be opened if you will help him succeed at conversation with you. A woman who gives her husband the gift of conversational clarity, third-object conversation, and pillow talk builds a bridge to her husband's heart that she can cross comfortably and safely for decades to come.

7

Friendship: The Secret Ingredient

This is my lover, this my friend.
SONG OF SONGS 5:16

———◆◆◆———

Even on the answering machine, I could hear the quiver in her voice. Something was very wrong. "Susan," Jessica said, "we really need to talk to you and Mark as soon as possible. Please call me?"

We returned the call immediately. "We just got your message. We're both on the phone. What's up?"

She responded with characteristic kindness: "I'm so sorry to bother you. I know how busy you are. How was your anniversary?"

"It was fine," I answered. Then, quickly changing the topic, I said, "We could tell by your message that something's really wrong. What's going on?"

Through quiet sobs, she explained, "I knew something

hasn't been right for months. Then tonight I found this folder of letters from a woman Jeff works with. He's admitted to everything, but he says he wants to change. What are we going to do?"

It was a long night—and a long year—as these two battled *together* to rebuild their marriage. There was no question they were willing to do whatever it took to get their marriage back on track. In addition to meeting with us, they attended a marriage enrichment retreat. They read books. They had double dates with other couples whose marriages they admired. But if you ask them today what saved their marriage, they'd say there was one decision that kept them hanging in there when they might otherwise have given up. What was it? It was the choice to build back *their friendship*.

I know. It sounds so unromantic, so simplistic. *What does rebuilding a friendship have to do with rescuing a marriage as troubled as Jessica and Jeff's?* you might be wondering.

The answer is *everything*.

Friendship: The Marriage-Saving Vaccine

University of Washington researcher John Gottman is what we call "a marriage inoculation specialist." He has brought a rigorous scientific approach to understanding what makes marriages work and what makes them fail. After years of observation and analysis, Gottman claims to be able to predict the future success or failure of the marriages he has observed with an accuracy rate of over *90 percent*. And usually, he says, he can make this determination within just a few minutes of observing a couple.

How does he do it? Gottman has discovered certain basic patterns that are marriage destroyers and others that are marriage protectors. And, far and away, the most significant marriage protector he has discovered is (are you ready to be underwhelmed?)—a couple's ability to be friends with each other:

> The determining factor in whether wives feel satisfied with sex, romance, and passion in their marriage is, by 70 percent, the quality of the couple's friendship. For men, the determining factor is, by the same 70 percent, the quality of the couple's friendship. So men and women come from the same planet after all. . . . Friendship fuels the flames of romance because it offers the best protection against feeling adversarial toward your spouse.[23]

In many ways building a friendship with your spouse is not a matter of learning new skills but simply accessing the ones you already have. Think back to our phone conversation with Jessica. Despite the fact that she was caught up in the emotions of anger and disappointment, she was able to put a hedge around those emotions and address *us* with her typical kindness and respect.

When it comes to conflicts between husbands and wives, we often assume that we *can't help* speaking to our spouses with disrespect and unkindness. Because I know my friend Jessica's personality well, I'm sure that the voice she was using with us ("I'm sorry to bother you. How was your anniversary?") was a voice long ago removed from her tone with her husband. She knew how to speak to us as friends but had forgotten how to do the same with Jeff.

The secret to healing this marriage was not to be found in an extravagant romantic getaway or in some revolutionary marriage-restoration breakthrough. It was going to be found in Jeff and Jessica relearning the principles of friendship that had come so naturally in the early years of courtship.

Friends Give Time: A Prescription for the Time-Starved Marriage

Check out any cereal box (or most packaged food items, for that matter), and you'll read about "minimum daily requirements" — amounts of certain vitamins, minerals, or fibers we need if we hope to stay healthy. Without these requirements being met, our bodies become anemic, weak, unable to fight off even a small infection.

If you want to keep your marriage healthy, if you want to develop the kind of friendship that can protect your marriage, it will take time. Time together. Without it, your marriage's immune system can become dangerously weak. And the little irritations that are a normal part of life will all too quickly become unmanageable.

Creating time to be together seldom comes without a fight—not against each other but against your schedules. The demands of work, volunteer opportunities, friends, extended family, even church can all pull you away from each other with a powerful force. Couples who simply go with the flow of their schedules may find that the underlying current does anything but draw them together. If there's any area of your marriage in which you'll need to be aggressive and intentional, it's in this area of ensuring that you make time to be together.

The Slot System

If Mark and I were sitting alongside you right now, he would pull out his Day-Timer and flip through the monthly calendar pages. You would find, on almost every week, little circled numbers scattered throughout; some days have three numbers circled; many days have none.

Mark perfected this practice after a series of very difficult conversations with me. When we were in our mid-twenties, I was painfully aware of my husband's tendency to jam-pack his schedule. I knew we could easily settle into a dangerous pattern of his saying yes to more and more opportunities and becoming less and less available for our marriage. Mark used to say, "It'll all work out. Don't worry about it." But I needed the security of a plan — a plan we could agree on *before* we drifted apart.

That's when we came up with the *slot system,* a process we've taught to hundreds of couples — a single strategy that has done more for keeping our marriage healthy than almost anything else we have done. It may sound a bit calculated and unromantic, but, like many recommendations for the first year of marriage, great marriages are built on the little choices normal couples tend to overlook.

Here's how the plan works: We look at our time together in one-week blocks, dividing each day into three distinct slots — morning, afternoon, and evening. Each slot has a meal, and each slot involves a block of time. A morning slot, for example, begins with waking up and ends around noon-time. The afternoon slot begins with lunch and ends around 5:00 P.M. The evening slot begins around 5:30 or 6:00 and ends at bedtime.

Over the years, we've learned that keeping our marriage healthy required a minimum of six slots together in a normal week. And the more unpredictable our schedules become, the more rigidly we need to practice the slot system. With this system, *you* get to rule your schedule and make your marriage a priority; without it, *your schedule* rules you, and your marriage loses by default. And that's exactly what was happening to Todd and Melanie.

Todd and Melanie had entered marriage with their eyes wide open to the challenges they would face. They were willing to do "whatever it takes" to make their marriage thrive. In fact, one of the agreements they had made in their premarital counseling two years earlier was that if their relationship ever got below "excellent," they would come in and talk with us—and that's why they were now sitting in Mark's office.

Melanie began. "Something's missing," she said. Todd nodded in agreement. "We entered marriage intending to dance together, but it feels like we're just plodding along, trying to make our marriage work."

Todd added, "It's like our car isn't running on all cylinders— like our wheels are turning without the bearings."

When we asked Todd and Melanie how they were doing in making time to be together, they both laughed—almost always a good sign in marriage counseling.

"What's so funny?" Mark asked.

"It's just nuts right now," Todd said. "What with starting a new business, I'm working late most nights. I typically get home around 8:00, and I'm exhausted. And that's when we get into our worst fights."

We asked about weekends. Melanie explained that Todd was working nearly every Saturday. She said they tried to grab some time together whenever they could. Most Sundays Melanie led the children's choir at church and Todd helped out with the youth group in the afternoon. "We've been good about having our date night on Saturday nights," Melanie added. "But lately, there's just been a lot of tension, even when we're doing something fun."

In a typical week, Todd and Melanie had only two slots together. Their schedule looked something like this:

Sunday	Monday	Tuesday	Wednesday	Thursday	Friday	Saturday
1. Church together	**W**	**O**	**R**	**K**	**!**	Todd works until 4:00 Mel and Todd Lunch
Youth Group 3:00–6:30 P.M.	**W**	**O**	**R**	**K**	**!**	Todd golfs with the guys
7:00 Mel's Junior League	Dinner at 8:30 after work	Dinner at 9:45 — after church mtg.	Dinner with Mel's parents at 7:00 (w/ or w/o Todd)	Dinner at 8:30 after work	Meet at the game for dinner	2. Date night

Todd and Melanie had forgotten the one thing this "newborn baby" marriage of theirs needed most: Time. *Quantity time* together does for marriage what an oil change does for a car. Of course, a car can go for a good while without an oil change before any problems become evident, but eventually the car starts to run sluggishly and unpredictably.

We asked Todd and Melanie to take a look at the upcoming week and select six slots when they could be together. Mark encouraged them *not* to think of these times simply in terms of one-on-one romantic getaways. These slots could be taken up with running errands together, watching TV, taking a nap, having dinner together with friends, or even just hanging around the house. The idea is that a couple carves out a basic number of no-pressure times to be available to be with each other.

As Mark explained the process, they swallowed hard. They knew their schedule would not easily yield to this kind of discipline. We suggested that if Todd had to work late, he could consolidate his times, so that he'd work until 10:00 o'clock one night and then come home by 5:30 the next evening. Or, instead of working 10:00 A.M. to 4:00 P.M. on Saturday, Todd could go in early and work 6:00 to 12:00, leaving two full slots for Todd and Melanie to be together.

Surprisingly, after only ten minutes of negotiating, Todd and Melanie came up with a plan for the week. Once they had picked their six slots, I drew five circles in their schedule. "These circles are a bonus," I said with a smile. "The beauty of the slot system."

Here's what their calendar looked like:

Sunday	Monday	Tuesday	Wednesday	Thursday	Friday	Saturday
1. Breakfast & church together	**W**	**O**	**R**	**K**	**!**	◯
◯	**W**	**O**	**R**	**K**	**!**	5. Home improvement projects
2. Youth Group at our house	◯	3. Dinner at home	◯	◯	4. Dinner with John and Louise	6. Date night

Every circle represents a slot when each partner is free to do something else—together or apart—without feeling the need to ask permission from the other. For example, with his circle times, Todd is free to work late, play golf, or watch a game with a group of friends. And he now has five slots outside of regular work hours in which to handle the extra workload that results from his new business. But he doesn't have to choose any longer between his business and his marriage. And with her circle times, Melanie is free to be purposeful about joining an investment club, writing a novel, or teaching an aerobics class—or, of course, the two of them might just wind up spending time just being together.

When Mark and I introduced this concept to our couples' group, they were startled by the idea that we were encouraging them to create these pockets of freedom throughout the week. They had assumed that, if they weren't spending every spare minute together, they were neglecting their marriages. Truth be told, couples who carve out *only* six slots a week actually tend to spend *more time* together than couples who say they spend all their discretionary time together. They are no longer giving each other the spare minutes — the leftovers — squeezed between their other activities. In reality, they're giving each other the *first* of their time and giving their work, hobbies, church, and friends what is leftover. Couples who put their six "together" slots in first — and then build the rest of their schedule around those slots — treat each other like million dollar clients, those people whose appointments with us we wouldn't dream of breaking.

Of course, this structure doesn't mean you no longer spend spare minutes, random lunches, or late-night dinners together. These unscheduled rendezvous can spice up your marriage, but with the slot system you no longer need to depend on them to provide the basic nutrients for your marriage.

Whenever Mark and I teach about the slot system, the question always seems to come up, "What about the times when six slots a week are simply impossible?" Given our erratic traveling schedule, we have more than a passing familiarity with this situation. Here's how it works for us: We "set the default button" at six slots per week. But when we have a week in which our time together dips below the normal level, we do our best to give ourselves *more* than six the next week. We realize that the health of our marriage requires it.

It's crucial to have this kind of system in place in the first year, especially before children come along. If you don't, it will be easy for you as a mother to shift the focus from your marriage to your children and to your other responsibilities.

As one wife confessed to me, "I was married to my job, to my children, to my volunteer work—anything but to my husband." It will be during the seasons of your life when you feel as though you have the *least* time to carve out time for your marriage that you will need it the most.

Friends Give Attention: It's Easier Than You Think

Both Mark and I grew up feeling at home in theater and music. But the dancing required in these shows sometimes pushed Mark out of his comfort zone. Many of the shows he was in would be professionally choreographed, and he would be expected to dance. The choreographer would stand in the front of this group of double-left-footed guys and say such encouraging things as, "It's simple. All you have to do is . . ." And with all the grace of startled frogs, they would attempt to follow the "simple" steps being taught—simple for the rhythmically gifted, of course; but for this pile of guys, it was anything but simple.

All too often, advice about marriage comes garbed in a false promise of simplicity. "The six easy steps" and "the seven simple secrets" are never nearly as easy and simple in real life as they are in the books. But we have stumbled upon a marriage-building process that is so simple, so boring, in fact, that almost anyone who can talk can succeed at it. You and your husband can use this no-brainer conversation method every time you are together.

Imagine this scene: You come into the kitchen for breakfast on an October Saturday morning, and your husband is engaged in his typical Saturday morning behavior—reading the paper, drinking his first cup of coffee. You exchange "good mornings," and he continues with what he's been doing. You also grab a cup of coffee. On your way to the kitchen table, you look out the kitchen window.

You: "Would you look at those leaves? They're incredible!"

Your husband (glancing over the paper and out the window): "Wow. They sure are." (He follows his comment with an affirmative "hmmm" sound.)

You: "I love this month." (Before you move to the table, you putter around the kitchen for a few minutes.)

Your husband: "Did you see that the Johnsons are selling their store?"

You (turning toward him momentarily and then back to puttering): "No kidding?"

Your husband: "Yeah."

You: "Hey, do you want to run to the hardware store with me after breakfast?"

Your husband: "Uh-huh."

Did you catch the drama, the tension, the passion? You're right, there isn't any. But when you read through the words of this conversation, I'll bet the one thing you *weren't* thinking was, "My husband and I could never do *that!*"

As unromantic as it may seem, this kind of dialogue, practiced on a regular basis, can make a huge difference in your marriage. No kidding. In fact, couples who talk like this regularly, who simply "turn toward each other," as Dr. Gottman puts it—with nods, glances, and even the affirmative grunts ("uh-huh")—are the ones who also report the strongest levels of romantic satisfaction.[24]

Believe it or not, these kinds of no-brainer conversations are the building blocks of friendship in marriage. More than the infrequent "deep talk," these simple, low-skilled exchanges, practiced thousands of times throughout your marriage, can build an ease with regard to being together. And with them you create a comfortable friendship that can protect your marriage against the things that could easily destroy it.

Friends Protect Their Friendship: The Destructive Power of Secrets

Six months into her marriage, Belinda discovered, quite by accident, that five years before she and Ralph were married, he had had an affair with a married woman, a colleague at work. Though the relationship had been over long before she and Ralph had ever met, Belinda simply couldn't let it go.

Finding no appropriate outlet for her fury, she found herself pushing him away, contemptuously punishing him by removing her affection, chastising him for not sharing this awful secret with her before the wedding, disrespecting him for his moral failure. Within six months, Ralph had given up. But after he filed for divorce, she changed her mind, begging Ralph to return to the negotiating table. He refused, and they were divorced less than a year after they had made their solemn vows.

As I watched their marriage unravel, I had to wonder. *Would things have been different if the secret had come out before the wedding?* I have to think so. I believe one of two things would have happened: Either the revelation of this past relationship would have driven such a wedge between them that they would never have gotten married, or she would have made the decision that she loved him enough to get past his past. Either way, they would have saved themselves the financial and emotional expense of a divorce. A broken engagement, though horrible, is not nearly as painful as a broken marriage.

I can think of very few situations in which anything is gained by deep secrets being kept from each other. Consequently—apart from confidential information related to your job (as a pastor, a lawyer, or a CIA agent) and apart from a situation in which you are married to someone who would threaten to harm you physically if they learned the truth about you (a much larger problem than your secret)—we urge couples to adopt a zero-secrets policy as they begin their marriages.

Friends Give Feedback: Four Sentences He'll Love to Hear

Sherri desperately wanted to build a lasting friendship with her husband, Bob. But every time she made a suggestion, Bob seemed to respond defensively—taking every comment as a personal attack, as though he was being judged a failure. Even though she'd often begin her comments with such words as "Why don't you just . . ." or "Have you ever thought about . . . ," she seemed to get nowhere.

It was clear from Bob's consistently negative reaction that Sherri had to try another approach. What she needed was a way to initiate nonthreatening conversations with her husband—the kind that comes naturally with friends. With the stealth of Sherlock Holmes and the dogged determination of Winston Churchill, she began asking friends and coworkers for ideas. Then she subjected each idea to the scientific method, taking each one home and trying it out on Bob.

Sherri discovered a couple things: First, she learned that it *was* possible to give marriage-building feedback to Bob without stirring up defensiveness in him, and second, she realized that when she found a sentence that worked, not only would Bob respond to her positively, but within a few weeks he would begin to use the very same sentence on her!

I was so fascinated by Sherri's story that I asked her for the list of sentences that actually worked with Bob. After learning her four "friendly feedback" sentences, it didn't take long for these to become a part of my regular vocabulary with Mark as well:

1. *"I like that!"* When your husband knows that he has brought you pleasure, he will become more confident, more playful, more likely to try out new ideas for bringing you happiness. A common frustration men voice about their marriages is that their wives are never satisfied, no matter what they do. "I like that!" will let him know that he has brought you satisfaction.

2. *"I don't know how you do it!"* With these words, you're presenting your husband with "the man of the year" trophy—communicating that you think he's an amazing person in all his pursuits, not just in what he does for you. When you notice that he's done something—anything—well, these words seal your membership in his fan club.

3. *"That counts."* These words give recognition that this man of yours has gone above and beyond the call of duty in order to show his love for you. When you catch him in the act of doing something ordinary or extraordinary—making the coffee in the morning, unloading the dishwasher, stopping by the bookstore and buying that novel you can't stop talking about—celebrate it with this affirmation. "That counts" will motivate him to think of more ways to demonstrate his love for you.

4. *"You know what I would just love?"* When you ask your husband for something in the language of pleasure rather than in the language of complaint, you are much more likely to get a pleasurable response. Using phrases such as "Can't you just once . . . ?" or "Why don't you ever . . . ?" always invites resistance and defensiveness. "You know what I would just love?" sets him up for an instant win.

Nothing can ensure the success of your marriage like simply knowing how to be friends with your husband. And friends, especially *best* friends, do a few simple things well. They spend time together, they pay attention to each other, they tell the truth, and they give encouraging feedback. Now, of course, you want something more than "just friendship" in your marriage. But it is only in the fields of friendship that the long-term passion and intimacy you long for can grow and flourish.

8

Conflict: Close Enough for Sparks to Fly

Despite what many therapists will tell you, you don't have to resolve your major marital conflicts for your marriage to thrive.

JOHN GOTTMAN, *THE SEVEN PRINCIPLES FOR MAKING MARRIAGE WORK*

We had been married for less than forty-eight hours. It was the first morning in our mountain honeymoon cottage. We had a leisurely breakfast, lounging around in the kind of plush bathrobes reserved only for honeymooners and movie stars. Looking out the window at the surrounding mountains, an aura of absolute contentment settled over us.

We sat comfortably close together, listening to the crackling of the fire. Eventually I got up to take a shower, while Mark stayed behind to tinker with the fire. But as I was singing under the stream of warm water, the thoughts running through my sweet husband's mind were far different from mine. Evidently the thought of his new bride in the shower awakened in Mark a creative idea he was sure we would never forget (I know *I* haven't!).

I was reveling in this luxurious, steaming shower, smiling over what a wonderful man I had married. I was singing songs—"Our Love Is Here to Stay" and "Can't Help Lovin' That Man of Mine." Awe and wonder enveloped me in the thought that this incredible man chose *me* to spend the rest of his life with. But everything changed in a split second.

Mark silently tiptoed into the bathroom to "make his memory." Out of nowhere, I received "the gift"—the result of his creative ruminations: a very large, very full, very icy pitcher of water dumped over me!

Forget the fact that one of the most popular movies that year was *Psycho,* featuring a terrifying attack on a woman in the shower. Forget the fact that I grew up with an older brother who took great joy in carrying out pranks like this one. Forget the fact that I *thought* that, now that I was married, I'd be safe from surprise attacks like "The Claw" (my brother Rick used to love watching Saturday night wrestling, and I was his favorite opponent). Oh, how naive I was!

Thoughts of honeymoon joy were quickly replaced by *"Who is this jerk anyway? He was so kind, so spiritual. How could I have not seen that this man is a psychopath? Aaaah!"*

I didn't laugh. I didn't chase him around the cottage in my shower suit. I didn't say anything. I just slumped down in the shower, ice cubes melting around my backside, and cried. When Mark leaned in to try to comfort me, he found a completely brokenhearted bride. "Leave me *alone!*" I snapped.

He had expected good-natured laughter, or a "very funny," or a "just you wait until *you* take a shower!" or maybe just a "hee-hee-hee; that was a good one."

As a college student, Mark and his roommates had played this kind of prank on each other all the time. It always gave them a good laugh and created some of that "male bonding" we've heard so much about. And since it bonded Mark so well to the guys, he just *knew* it was going to be a great hit with me as well.

Bad idea.

After I thawed out and regained my composure and got dressed, we sat for a long time. Groveling and saying how sorry he was, Mark listened as I told him how terrified and hurt I felt. We learned a lot that day about the inevitability of conflict in marriage. We learned that, though conflict may come accidentally and carelessly, resolution only comes through purposeful hard work.

When you dream about marriage, I doubt very much that disappointment, disagreements, and shower-terror make it into your dreams. You aren't thinking about the ways this man you love will conspire to irritate you. Know this, though: he will. And if you want the kind of intimacy with your husband you've always longed for, it will only come from knowing how to handle conflict together.

Welcome to the Roller Coaster

Our family loves roller coasters. Let me take that back. Everyone in our family loves roller coasters — except Mark. He's the guy who steps off Mr. Toad's Wild Ride with a face as green as asparagus. But because he likes to hang out with the people in our family, he frequently finds himself stepping into clanking little cars on greasy, twisting tracks and traveling at speeds and angles that leave his stomach wishing it were somewhere else.

These rides always include the familiar triple and quadruple safety checks. Of course, the wilder the ride, the more harnesses and straps there are and the more snugly your head is held in place. After my first roller-coaster ride, I never questioned why those people dressed in spacesuits spend so much time making sure everyone is locked in. They know that without safety harnesses, someone could die.

Marriage may just be the wildest ride you'll ever take. The turns are unpredictable; the spins can be incredibly uncomfortable. And at times, the only thing you may be able to think about is *when can I get off this thing?* So before you begin the ride, check to make sure all safety mechanisms are in place and working. The time to discover that your seat belt doesn't work isn't when you're dangling upside down a hundred feet off the ground.

We've found three safety checks you can use to protect your marriage from the dangerous twists and turns of disappointment, discouragement, and hurt. If you're strapped in securely, you may discover that conflict actually becomes an invitation to deeper intimacy—and can even be fun as well.

Safety Check #1: Conflict Will Happen

There is only one surefire way to guarantee you will never fight with your husband: Don't get married.

Go ahead, strive for the marriage you've always dreamed of. Strive for an exceptional, uncommon life together. Strive to love each other more deeply each year. But give up on the expectation that if you somehow "do it right" you will "get out of jail free" and never have to face the irritation, disappointment, and discouragement over the way your husband has handled a particular situation or failed to do what he promised to do when you got married.

Conflict *will* happen—guaranteed. You will not be able to predict what the specific nature of the conflict will be, but you *can* be prepared for the disagreements that are sure to come.

Maybe your husband is a morning person, and you're a night person. He goes to bed early and calls for you to join him. You say you'll be there in a minute but spend the next thirty minutes putzing around the kitchen, and his frustration begins to boil. And by the time you finally make it upstairs to join him, the fuse on the powder keg has already been lit. The spontaneous combustion catches you off guard.

Maybe your husband is the king of spontaneity, and you are a neat freak. His drinking glasses will, before long, make permanent rings on your coffee table. You've asked him again and again to use coasters. For the first few weeks of your marriage, you didn't mind cleaning up after him, but now the more of his messes you clean up, the more frustrated you become. One day he walks in the door and discovers that your tolerance has just come to a fiery end.

I can't predict where the hair trigger will be on your conflicts, but I know the conflicts will come.

Safety Check #2: Prepare to Forgive

To some people, forgiveness sounds so easy—so, well, nice. But forgiveness is tough. It isn't for cowards. There is nothing effortless about it. It can, in fact, present the most demanding challenge of your entire marriage.

But when you do not forgive your husband for the hurt or disappointment he has caused you, you lock yourself in a prison and wait for your husband to find the key. Creating a list of demands he must meet before he can be forgiven will only keep *you* behind bars. I have seen women who stay "locked up"—emotionally, sexually, vocationally, spiritually—burning with bitterness for years. Ironically, you're the one who has the most power to bring healing. Your forgiveness can neutralize the corrosive effects of your husband's blunders.

If you want a safe ride on this wild adventure, be prepared to forgive this man.

Safety Check #3: Do You Have Your Fire Extinguishers Handy?

Now let's get practical. You've resigned yourself to the fact that conflict in your marriage is inevitable; you're prepared to forgive this man who won't always get it right. We want you armed with the most powerful strategies available for reducing and overcoming the conflicts.

These secrets — "fire extinguishers," so to speak — have been proven to snuff out the fires of conflict — those burning, painful, thoughtlessly spoken words and reactions that have the potential to explode like a stick of dynamite. Where do these secrets come from?

Once again we turn to Dr. Gottman. What I love about his approach is that these strategies for overcoming conflicts are more than just good ideas; they are the very ones used by couples who *have* built happy and satisfying marriages. One of his most significant findings was that focusing on communication skills and on active listening — techniques recommended by most marriage counselors — are seldom helpful in handling conflict. These techniques quickly get forgotten once a couple becomes embroiled in an emotional conflict.

So get ready. You just may be surprised at how simple these "fire extinguishers" are.

Complain; Don't Criticize

Dr. Gottman makes this observation: "There is no such thing as constructive criticism. All criticism is painful. Unlike complaints — specific requests for change — criticism doesn't make marriage better. It inevitably makes it worse."[25] A complaint is focused on a specific issue—a *specific request* for change. Raising a concern typically will not have any adverse effect on the happiness of a marriage. Criticism, on the other hand, converts a concern into an attack.

Here are a few examples:

- *Complaint:* "I wish you would take out the trash!"

  Criticism: "How many times do I have to ask you to do something as simple as taking out the trash? Why can't you remember to help out around here?"

- *Complaint:* "Don't you think we need to carve out some time for us? It's been a long time since we went on a date."

  Criticism: "You seem to have *plenty* of time for your buddies. What about me? When do I get some of that attention? No more nights out for you until we have a date."

- *Complaint:* "It hurts me when you don't hold my hand in public. It makes me think you're ashamed of me."

  Criticism: "Why won't you show me any affection in public? All you care about is keeping up your image. What's the matter? Are you afraid people will think that you love me?"

In the heat of the moment, when your emotions have percolated to the surface because of genuine frustration, it's difficult to say the right thing every time. But you *can* keep from globalizing your concern into a criticism. Stick to the infraction.

When the Flood Comes, Take a Break

Watch a tennis match on television sometime. What happens when a player disagrees with a call? Go to a baseball game and see what happens when the manager argues with the umpire — two grown men screaming at the top of their lungs, their noses no more than three inches apart.

Their anger is like a flood. As they become consumed by the emotions of conflict, they can no longer deal with it in a productive way. When a man "gets flooded" during a conflict, he may just shut down to a sullen silence, grunting out a "fine," a "who cares," or a "whatever." Or he may go into an attack mode and shout out with defensiveness and contempt, "I said it was fine! What more do you want from me?"

No, it's not your imagination. According to the research, "It's a biological fact that men are more easily overwhelmed by marital conflict than their wives are. It is harder for a man's body to calm down after an argument than a woman's."[26] Many wives, though, make a critical mistake by *continuing* their complaint even after their husbands have become flooded. Because women are the ones who will bring up problems — more than 80 percent of the time — their tendency is to be unwilling to let them go.[27] And because women feel a greater ownership of the problem, they also tend to have more tolerance for enduring the conflict.

When you or your husband gets flooded in a conflict, the best thing to do is to recognize that you're wasting your time and simply take a break. In one love lab experiment, researchers interrupted couples in the heat of conflict, explaining that the staff needed to make some adjustments to the microphones. The researchers simply asked the couples to wait for twenty minutes before returning to their previous conversation. And in *every* case, heart rates had gone down, "floods" had subsided, and couples were able to deal with the conflict more productively.[28]

Start Arguments Softly

- *Soft Start-Up:* "Can we talk for a minute about the trip we're about to take to my mother's house?"

   Harsh Start-Up: "Every time we visit my mom, you act like such a spoiled brat."

- *Soft Start-Up:* "What's the possibility that we could renegotiate the chores around the house?"

   Harsh Start-Up: "Let me tell you something. I'm not your mother. I'm not your slave. And I'm tired of waiting on you hand and foot!"

The research is absolutely conclusive that the introductory moments of a conflict have everything to do with its outcome. If you begin every confrontation with thoughtful words and a pleasant face, your chances for a satisfying outcome are wonderfully improved. If you charge into conflicts with your head down and your nostrils flaring, your matador will respond the only way he knows how.

When Bobbie's friend Peg was first married, she and Grant held "fireside chats" every Friday evening. They asked each other, "Is there anything I did this week that bothered you?" The setting was calm and serene. Emotions were completely in check.

"It really bugs me when you drive over the reflectors in the middle of the road on purpose," Peg admitted. Grant did this just for the fun of it and had no idea it was a sore spot, and he thanked her for letting him know.

Peg could have attacked him while his tires were thumping their annoying cadence. "That noise is driving me crazy. Can't you stay in your lane like everyone else?" Because Peg practiced a soft start-up, a conflict was avoided; a problem was solved.

Don't Expect to Resolve Every Conflict

There are two very different kinds of conflict in a marriage—solvable and perpetual. And you may be surprised—or disappointed—to learn that almost 70 percent of conflicts fall into the *perpetual* category.[29] These are usually personality tendencies and quirky habits that are not threatening to your marriage. The majority of perpetual issues we argue about in our marriage will simply not be solved, issues such as these:

- Dana loves parties and wishes that Walter wasn't so shy and quiet in a group.
- Donald is a strict disciplinarian and wants Rena to be firmer with their son; Rena thinks Donald should lighten up.
- Anita is extremely frugal and likes to have plenty of cash in reserve; Cliff thinks nothing of spending money, especially on risky ventures.
- Jim loves to work out and won't miss a day of exercise; Sally hates the thought of breaking a sweat and doesn't understand his obsession.
- Bobbie is a free spirit who sometimes leaves the dish towel lying haphazardly on the counter; Robert can't walk through the kitchen without straightening it out.
- Mark hates the television and believes that it will turn our children's brains to broccoli; I enjoy watching television and wish Mark would slow down and watch it with me.

I was amazed to discover that couples can actually live happily together with unresolved conflicts. In fact, in our work with couples, we used to spend an inordinate amount of effort trying to get couples to resolve all their conflicts, usually with minimal success.

The next time you're talking to a veteran couple—one you consider to be happily married—ask them if they're dealing with some perpetual conflict that has been an issue for them for their whole marriage. I have little doubt that they will say yes. Satisfied couples have simply found ways to dance with the conflict issues that don't seem to budge.

When it comes to television in our home, I doubt that Mark and I will ever agree. He would be happy to see all televisions donated to science—definitely not given away to the poor, because no one should have to endure the "brain-rotting effects of this spawn of Satan." I, on the other hand, grew up with the television on almost perpetually. And though our family watches only a fraction of what I did growing up, I do love it when our family spends an occasional evening together watching TV. When we're sitting in the nursing home forty years from now, Mark will probably still think we're wasting our time in front of the television. I'll still be saying, "Shhhh! This is the best part!"

Do the Patch Work

A strategically placed patch can salvage an otherwise useless thing. A dress, a pair of jeans, or a punctured tire can be restored with this kind of simple repair. When your conflict with your husband spirals into a negative or destructive place, you can patch it with a statement or gesture that deescalates the battle and restores your relationship.

When things got a little tense between my parents, my dad used to smile and say to my redheaded mom, "I love it when your face gets the color of your hair." Mark and I have come up with our own patch that seems to resolve at least most of our petty conflicts: I get to be right on the odd days of the month, and Mark gets to be right on the even days. When we are arguing about directions or about what time Mark said he'd be home, one of us will interrupt the fight with "what's the date today?" We let the calendar decide who's right.

But patches don't all need to be silly. It can be a simple statement such as "I can see your point" or "Wow! I've been completely missing what you were saying." The key to successful patching is the receiving spouse. When your husband offers a patch, even if it's not perfect, you have a choice. You can either keep pounding your point, which may result in your husband becoming flooded and increasingly resistant. Or you can join him with some patch work of your own.

I'll never forget the story our friends Rusty and Betty told us about a car trip they had taken. After an erupting conflict, they settled into an uncomfortable, icy silence. Ten minutes into the silence, Rusty decided to play. He didn't realize at the time that it was a patch, but it clearly was. As they passed an unusually large pack of mules, he said brightly, "Relatives of yours?" At this point Betty had a choice. She could maintain the tension (and perpetuate the misery of their trip) or she could match her husband's levity. She chose the latter and said, "Why, yes. On my husband's side, of course." A willingness to risk this kind of playfulness *and to receive it* from each other has a delightful way of keeping us majoring on our love and minoring on our conflict.

And just in case you're keeping score: Over the past twenty-three years, I've had the chance to bless my husband with enough of my own "good morning, camper!" pitchers of ice water in the shower. Hee-hee-hee.

I know I'm right—it's an odd-numbered day!

9

Money: The Other Lover

Money is a wonderful thing, but it's possible to pay too high a price for it.

ANONYMOUS

 group of men had finished their workout and were talking in the locker room. A cell phone interrupted their conversation. One of the guys picked it up and checked the caller I.D. The preprogrammed message read "Your Wife." Glancing around the locker room, he flipped it open and said hello.

The woman's voice on the other end of the phone was enthusiastic. She didn't waste any time with pleasantries. "Honey," she said, "you know how we've been looking at cars?"

With a skeptical hesitation, he answered slowly, "Uh-huh."

"Well, I think I've found the perfect one. It's a little more than what we wanted to spend, but you are going to love it!" Her words were ecstatic, punctuated by rapid breaths as she continued, "It's a little red Mercedes convertible. The sticker price is $53,000, but I think they can do better than that, don't you?"

He paused for a moment. "That sounds like a fair price to me. I'd go ahead and give them what they're asking. I just want you to be happy."

He could tell she was beaming as she answered, "I'll buy it right now."

"Sounds great. Have a great day!" He closed the flap on the phone and looked around the locker room.

With a mischievous grin he called out, "Hey, anybody know whose phone this is?"

When It's Your Money, It's Not That Funny

I've learned a good general rule: When conversations about money come this easily in my marriage, I want to be sure it's really my husband I'm talking to! In real life, dealing with money can present some of the greatest challenges that your marriage will ever face.

According to research, nearly 70 percent of married women list money as the number one stressor in their families.[30] And the Gallup organization has documented that financial pressure is, hands down, the number one problem faced by families. Not particularly surprising. What *is* surprising is that there isn't even a close second. While most respondents agreed that financial stress was the biggest challenge, the second-place answer (health and health care concerns) received only 6 percent of the votes.

In the light of the pressure put on the normal marriage by finances, it is surprising how many couples are not prepared for the challenges they are certain to face. In fact, only about 1 out of every 10 of the couples we work with has even begun a budget. Before saying "I do," most couples treat the warnings about future financial challenges in the same way they may treat a flight attendant's safety instructions.

I wonder, *What if all airplane passengers knew there was a better than 50 percent chance that they would actually be using the floatation devices beneath them or the oxygen masks neatly concealed above them?* I don't know about you, but I'd be listening pretty carefully to the preflight instructions.

The Single-Mind Principle

There are all kinds of reasons couples avoid financial preparation. The idealist says, "Money problems will take care of themselves if we love each other enough." The passive-aggressive spouse says, "When it comes to money, I just smile and nod and buy whatever I want." The avoidance specialist says, "Money always makes us fight, so we just don't talk about it anymore."

More often than not, couples who don't talk about finances slip into quiet standoffs that keep everybody unhappy. Few issues can eat away at the fabric of a marriage like a husband and a wife who have different unspoken expectations about finances. What you need are a few steps to help you and your husband structure your finances in a way that keeps both of you on the same side of the table.

Our Money

Start with the agreement that, after the marriage, all of your income will go into a single pot called "our money." Moving 100 percent of your income into a single pile prevents a number of unnecessary and potentially explosive conflicts:

- You avoid arguments over who is responsible to pay which bills.

- You no longer have "his and her" funds and bills that can easily lead to patterns of blaming and finger-pointing.
- It puts you together on the same side of the table as you creatively address the many financial challenges of your marriage.
- Your egos will be less threatened in the event that one of you makes a lot more money than the other.

The Marriage Insurance Premium

So far, so good. But what happens when one of you takes some of "our money" and spends it on something that the spouse would see as foolish? You may be convinced that a new $350 juicer is an absolute necessity; your husband may be equally convinced that paying $500 for a new set of golf clubs is a much higher priority. As crazy as it sounds, issues of no less consequence have unraveled the trust of many marriages.

To prevent this kind of predicament, we've developed a secret we like to call the *Marriage Insurance Premium* (or MIP). It works like this: At the beginning of each month, one of the first bills you pay out of "our money" is your MIP. There are no commissions, no agencies; in fact, you pay the money to yourselves, giving each of you absolute power over a bit of money each month.

The MIP need not be the same for each of you. For example, you and your husband may agree that you will receive $100 a month and he will receive $50 a month. You can take your money and put it in a mutual fund or save it up and buy the juicer; your husband can put his toward a new Nike driver. The only rule is that neither of you can criticize the MIP expenditures of the other.

With this arrangement, each of you gets to make a few unilateral decisions without creating a conflict. We call it marriage *insurance,* because it protects you from potentially destructive conflicts over money—and it's much cheaper than marriage counseling or a divorce.

The Spending Plan

Once you've allowed the MIP to create enough space for your financial idiosyncrasies, you're ready to develop your spending plan. I like the term *spending plan*—what you *can* spend money on—much better than *budget*—what you *can't* spend money on.

The secret cannot be reduced to making more money. The insurance industry tells us that large sums of money paid out to beneficiaries are typically gone in *six months*. The same is true for lottery winners.

As we've watched couples who become wealthy, nearly all of them shaped their spending plan with the same two priorities in view: giving and saving. Couples who agree on these two priorities often find that the process of determining the rest of their spending plan comes much more easily. Though your circumstances may require different percentages, the simplest strategy is summed up in this formula:

- Give 10 percent.
- Save 10 percent for the long haul (retirement and children's college expenses).
- Save 10 percent for the short haul (purchasing cars or furniture or carrying out major home improvements).

- Allot 70 percent for "Our Money"—including the Marriage Insurance Premiums, out of which bills are paid.

We picture the total process like this:

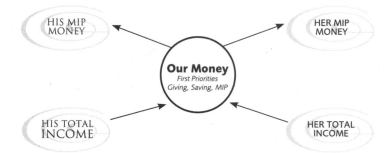

As you build your spending plan, start by listing, month by month, all your sources of income, including your paycheck, your husband's paycheck, gifts, and your investment income. Then make a list of all the expenses you can think of and put them into categories: giving, savings, MIPs, housing (rent or mortgage), utilities, car expenses, clothing, groceries, travel, telephone, donations, magazine subscriptions, personal (haircuts, dry cleaning), insurance, home decor, gifts, and miscellaneous expenditures.

From this point, you have both moved to the same side of the table in determining how much to allot for each spending category.

Money Attitudes That Murder Marriages

Money itself never causes conflict in marriage. What escalates into money fights are the unspoken *attitudes* you and your groom bring into your marriage. As a wife, there are two mind-sets that will hurt you every time:

"Money Is My Husband's Department"

Albert and Jennifer were financially comfortable when they first got married. Both had high-profile jobs that provided generous incomes. In fact, Jennifer had been so successful that she had over $100,000 in savings when they got married. After the wedding, Albert took care of everything related to the money—the insurance, the investments, the bill-paying. He made almost every financial decision, and she experienced great comfort in not having to worry about it.

When their first child was born, Jennifer wanted to stay at home. Albert agreed that they could swing it financially, and they continued in their familiar lifestyle. Then Albert lost his job. Through it all, he assured Jennifer that they would be fine. Asking no questions, she kept her spending at her normal level.

Albert was able to land a few short-term consulting jobs, but as he moved into the third year without employment, trouble began. He began putting restrictions on Jennifer's spending, and she began asking questions. What she discovered shocked and terrified her: Over the course of the past two years, they had spent their entire savings. And they were currently living on loans.

Jennifer had thought she was being a good wife, supporting her husband and not asking questions. Albert had tried to protect Jennifer by keeping the bad news at bay in hopes of a turnabout. Both were trying to do the right thing—trying to show love for each other. But this arrangement left Albert carrying a heavy weight he was never supposed to carry alone and left his wife with the devastation of feeling betrayed.

Couples who wait to talk about finances until there's a problem set themselves up for conflict from which they may never recover. As much as you may think it's preventing discomfort early in your marriage, it's never helpful to abdicate the responsibility for decisions about what to do with "our money."

"It's Easier to Ask for Forgiveness Than Permission"

Bobbie has a friend who lives by the shopping motto "Never leave a paper trail." As often as possible, Jeri avoids using checks or credit cards so that her husband will never know where she's been spending her money.

The crazy thing is that Jeri really has very little to hide. She's not running a drug-smuggling ring; she's not gambling on the side. She's only buying a few extra things for herself, for the house, and even a few surprises for her husband. She loves the freedom of being able to buy these things without "asking for permission." Her small consulting practice provides enough of "her own money" to do this undetected.

Jeri has a legitimate need to have this freedom to make some discretionary financial decisions herself. She wants to be treated like an adult. But the naked truth is that she doesn't trust her husband enough to come openly to the table to talk about what she's doing. Her "ask for forgiveness rather than permission" approach sets the stage for secrets, for distrust, and for hiding—a pattern that can easily find its way into other areas of their relationship.

Wise Women's Words

I've done an informal survey of married women about the subject of money. I asked them, "If you could say just one thing to new brides about how to build the right kind of pattern for dealing with money, what would it be?" Consider these tips as sage advice from the front lines:

"It's Not Unromantic or Unspiritual to Pay Attention to Money"

You don't have to read far into the New Testament to discover that God cares deeply about your attitudes related to money. There are five times more references in the New Testament to money than to prayer. You can add up the Bible's every reference to heaven or hell, and you'll still wind up with less material than you'll find related to money. And you may be surprised to know that, of Jesus' thirty-eight parables, sixteen relate to money in some way.

You may think that spending a romantic evening together or sharing a deep conversation about spiritual things will lead to satisfying intimacy. But neglecting conversation with your husband about money often puts up an obstacle to this intimacy. The earlier and clearer your conversations about money, the freer you'll be to pursue the things that matter most.

"There's Nothing You Need Badly Enough Right Now to Go into Debt for It"

By recent estimates, the typical household in America has $23,000 in nonmortgage debt. If we assume a moderate interest rate of 10 percent for that debt, the average couple is paying about $2,300 a year in interest alone. If a young couple would choose to avoid nonmortgage debt and put the $2,300 a year into savings, they could have, after twenty years of marriage, a nest egg in the neighborhood of $100,000, depending on the interest rate. Without spending a penny more than the average couple already spends on interest alone, you and your husband could have the many options this kind of money brings.

Too many couples leverage their future in order to buy a few more things they just have to have right now. The strain that a high debt load places on a marriage can be immense. Particularly during this first year, it's very important to live free from nonmortgage debt.

Asim and Colleen employ what they call their "walk-away principle." They agree to go home and leave any item over $200 in the store for twenty-four hours. If one of them "just loved it" the day before, it may not be as enticing the next day. With the passion removed, the couple can decide if the item is a "need" or a "want."

"If You Want to Live on One Income Someday, Live on One Income Now"

Anna and Andrew got married in their mid-twenties, knowing that one day they'd want to start a family. Early in their relationship they decided that Anna would not work outside the home once the children came. As a two-career couple, they lived at the level at which they could afford to live. Before the children arrived, they grew accustomed to new cars, a house with a large mortgage, frequently eating out, and annual high-dollar vacations.

Midway through their fourth year of marriage Anna became pregnant, and they realized the rough ride they had set themselves up for. When they looked at what their spending plan would be, based on only one salary, they were shocked at what it was going to cost to have a baby *and* to be a stay-at-home mom. Faced with the decision of vastly decreasing their standard of living or abandoning the decision for Anna to stay home with the baby, they made the difficult choice and severely cut back on their lifestyle. Putting a for-sale sign in their front yard was a painful reminder of their poor planning.

It would have been far easier if Anna and Andrew had learned to live on one income during the first few years of their marriage. They would have had three years of Anna's salary in savings—a cushion that could have *increased* their standard of living when the baby came.

So Where Do We Begin?

We met with Mike and Lynn several times before their wedding. In addition to regularly scheduled premarital sessions, they asked for special help in overcoming their frustrating pattern of tension with regard to money matters. They were wise enough to see that this pattern would set them up for a lifetime of frustration. And so, even before their wedding, these two resolved to build a different set of patterns. They knew that the marriage they've dreamed of would never be possible as long as they couldn't talk about money without becoming resentful.

One of the things we loved about working with this couple was their willingness to keep trying until they found a strategy that worked. In the first place, they did the kinds of things you've read about in this chapter—like creating a budget and establishing a monthly MIP. They even took a class on financial planning. They also tried some wild ideas—their own patented money dance they agreed to do every time they felt tension creeping into their ordinary money talks, and the special song—complete with motions—that they could never get through completely without laughing. And for a while they agreed to wear clown noses every time they talked about money. (I'm not kidding you.)

Now, ten years into their marriage, they would tell you that no single money strategy "worked." What did work was their uncompromising commitment to work a plan together, their absolute willingness to rid themselves of the corrosive oppositional patterns that elevated money above their marriage.

So where do *you* begin? How about resolving during this year to establish a pattern that allows the two of you to talk and negotiate about money without the tension and self-destructive seriousness that so often accompanies couples' financial conversations? Begin by agreeing that you will stay on the same team, sit on the same side of the table, and make your first priority not just solving a particular money issue but doing so in such a way that money never drives a wedge between you and your husband.

10
Sex: Better Than Chocolate

Marital sex can never prove enduringly suc-
cessful for a man until his wife gets her most
central needs satisfied.

NEIL CLARK WARREN, CATCHING THE RHYTHM OF LOVE

———◦◦◦———

*I*t started out like most days for Nick. He was out the
door and on his way to work an hour or two before
Cathy woke up. As he dressed for the day, his desire
to climb back under the covers with his newlywed bride was
intense, but he thought better of it. Cathy had been exhausted
lately from her new job. Nick reasoned that the last thing she
needed was to wake up to her overly amorous husband pawing
all over her. Taking care not to disturb her, he left and focused
his thinking on the night they'd spend together when he got
home.

Throughout the day, Nick had many sexual thoughts.
These were brought on by a glance at an attractive woman,
suggestive clothing, or even a kind and encouraging word
from a female coworker. It didn't take much. Sometimes just

a magazine cover, a billboard, or a random song on the radio was enough. At times he found himself thinking about sex for no apparent reason at all.

Nick was not a sex addict. He was a man committed to living with integrity. He was deeply in love with his wife and committed to "fidelity of the mind." And so he had made the decision that, instead of letting his mind linger on a person or image that might have prompted sexual thoughts, he would always seek to redirect those thoughts exclusively toward his bride.

At 6:00 P.M. he begins his drive home. He imagines a night of lovemaking with his bride. Out of faithfulness to his wife, he may have daydreamed about this scene ten times or more throughout the day. But the second he walks through the door, he realizes that his mind's trip to Fantasy Island is over.

Cathy greets him at the door with an unemotional hello and an immediate reminder that he had forgotten to take the trash out. "We missed the garbage man, and our trash cans are full." As they walk toward the living room, she lets him know that his sweaty jogging clothes are still right where he left them — in the middle of the walk-in closet.

Despite her obvious frustration with him, he goes ahead and hugs her, attempting a brief but sincere kiss. She pulls away, shoots him a disapproving look, and says, "Don't start getting any ideas."

Nick is thinking, "Start *getting any ideas? I've been having these ideas since 5:00 this morning!*" He gives up and trudges into the den, slumps into his chair, picks up the remote, and sits in stony silence.

It doesn't have to be this way. A woman who seeks to understand her husband sexually, who sees his sexual interest in her as a marker of faithfulness rather than of selfishness, is far more likely to experience full and satisfying intimacy. But sustaining this kind of incredible, mutually satisfying sex life will most likely not come naturally.

Without question, moments of sexual ecstasy are normal in any marriage. But you want more than a few moments. You want a sexual *lifestyle* with your husband that is consistently, even increasingly, satisfying for both of you. And it all begins with understanding yourself.

The Whiplash Effect

For a young woman who has guarded her heart and her bed and who enters marriage with the gift of no experience, to make the change from being the virgin bride to being her husband's sexual playmate can be more than a little challenging. Happily, we know far more about how to get ready for sex than Queen Victoria, who passed on this bit of wedding-night wisdom to all of her soon-to-be-married daughters: "Close your eyes, grit your teeth, and pray for the Empire."[31]

For years, turning *off* your sexual desires may have been the way you demonstrated faithfulness to God and to your future husband. But now, this same faithfulness invites the exact opposite response. So don't be surprised if you experience an unsettling whiplash effect during this first year, as you move from a habit of saying "no. No! NO!" into a pattern of "yes. Yes! YES!"

Sex is not simply about satisfying your *husband's* needs. It is a free-falling, rollicking, best-friend fun that can invite the childlike nature of you and your husband to "come out and play"—the most natural form of holy play a couple can experience together. Couples who have the richest intimacy, the greatest resilience, the most contagious sense of joy, are those who have learned lightheartedness at a *child to child* level.

In premarital counseling, we say to couples that if there isn't plenty of play in their lovemaking, they're missing the point. Great sex in marriage is not primarily about "getting it right"; it's more about fumbling and bumbling around together until you laughingly stumble upon those things that bring the greatest satisfaction and joy.

Learning early in your marriage to see sex as a no-pressure playground can prepare you for those times when sex may feel more like work than play. If you don't cultivate a spirit of playfulness in your marriage, the typical encounters with your overly amorous husband can easily lead to resentment and anger. When I see my husband's advances not as demands for performance but as affirming invitations to laugh together, I am free to say, as one tired, disheveled bride said to her husband on a day when she felt anything but attractive, "You've *obviously* got incredible taste in women."

I love to watch animal shows on television. Whether it's the guy with the crocodiles or someone talking about out-of-control adolescent elephants, these shows always capture my attention. Not long ago, I was watching a special on otters and monkeys, and there was one sentence I heard that will always stick with me: *It is always the most intelligent animals that know how to play.* The same is true for us. We are at our best, our most intelligent—in marriage, at work, in life—when we have learned how to play. And in marriage, sex is the grand playground.

Now, when I describe sex as play, some women assume that I am talking about "slap and tickle" games or jumping raucously on the bed. Uhhh—not necessarily. Truth be told, when it comes to this very vulnerable area of our lives, women like you and me want to be taken seriously; we want to be spoken to with quiet words of romance and cherishing respect.

One warning: Women who have been sexually abused will undoubtedly experience difficulty stepping into this kind of holy play. These women can carry a grave resistance to their husband's sexual invitations. A woman with this kind of history may struggle sexually with her husband because *she's* dealing with something that is beyond his control. If this describes you, don't let your past prevent you from enjoying the sexual intimacy with your husband you were made to enjoy. By seeking the help of a qualified Christian counselor early in your marriage, you can experience healing and move on to satisfying intimacy with your husband.[32]

Getting to What You Want: You Are His Only Teacher

Even though we aren't stuck with Queen Victoria's attitude, far too many women resign to endure sex rather than enjoy it. I saw this resignation in the young bride who asked me, "I'm just wondering—how often am I really going to have to do this?"

Maybe you have no trouble affirming the goodness of sex—and maybe the whiplash effect will have a limited effect on you. Perhaps you'll struggle with a different problem. You may have difficulty finding sex consistently satisfying.

I've got some good news and some bad news for you:

- The good news is that your husband *can* learn to bring you great pleasure in sex.
- The bad news is that *you* have to be the one to teach him.

And here's a little more good news and bad news:

- The good news is that you will have little difficulty finding out what satisfies him.
- The bad news is that it will take your husband a lot of effort to understand and practice the things that bring you pleasure.

During our engagement, Mark and I read a Christian book about sex. One of the chapters promised to give "The Key to Feminine Sexual Response." Soon after we were married, I discovered two things about sex: (1) My husband was determined to master that "key" and use it with monotonous frequency, and (2) on my excitement scale, that technique ranked just below watching oatmeal boil—in spite of what the book said!

Maybe this picture from the world of sports will help you understand your husband a little better. When it comes to sex, the only game your husband may know how to play well is baseball. And unless you teach him otherwise, his game will look something like this:

- He will touch the same three bases as quickly as possible—in the same predictable order,
- then he will rush for home.

Running the bases may come naturally to your Babe Ruth, but it won't feel much like a home run to you.

Men—the sexually predictable gender—have the ironic ability to think about *sex* all the time but seldom ever *think* about sex. Many husbands simply assume that their wives have the same approach to sex that they do—but we wives can be anything but predictable.

What is even more confusing for your husband is that

you may want such different things at different times. I know there are times when I want my back massaged or my feet rubbed or my hair brushed. Sometimes I want a long gourmet encounter; at other times, the last thing I want is a forty-five minute WWF (World Wrestling Federation) main event, and a quick romp is more the order of the day. Although I happen to be married to one of the most loving and creative men in the world, I'm pretty sure he'd get it wrong almost every time without clear signals from me.

So be prepared to teach your husband *your* version of baseball—with rules that go something like this:

> Start out in the batter's box and take a nice slow jog to first base. Once you get there, just touch it for an instant, turn around and head back to the batter's box for a few practice swings. Then jog out to left field, pick some flowers, and come back to the batter's box again and just sit and talk about the game for a few minutes. Take a few more pitches, and head straight for second base as fast as you can—but don't stay there long. Take a jog over the pitcher's mound right back to the batter's box one more time. Once you get there, swing as hard as you can, and when you make contact, run directly to third base. I'll be your third base coach. You'll just have to watch for my signals—I may want you to stay on base, head back to first, or run for home like there's no tomorrow! If you'll listen to me, you will score. But more important than that, the next time you invite me to play, I'll be humming the tune to "Take me out to the ball game!"

Trust me on this one: The chances of your husband just "figuring you out" sexually are about as likely as him figuring out what you want him to pick up at the grocery store without a list.

So, during this first year, your mission is to teach your husband how to please you and how to satisfy you. Help him become an expert on helping *you* enjoy sex. But, of course, teaching him how to satisfy you sexually requires that you become aware of what pleases you—a process that may feel like sailing uncharted waters. Just relax. The first year of marriage ought to be the worst year of sex you'll ever have. Don't stress out over having great sex during this year; you've got the rest of your life to work on it. You wouldn't expect to pick up a new language after your first conversation in a foreign land. Let this be a year of experimenting and learning about each other. God has designed human sexual intimacy in such a way that you can successfully bring each other pleasure—even if you don't quite know what you are doing yet.

In this first year, you may need to ask your husband to begin with a time of nonsexual touching before moving into foreplay. You need to specifically tell him exactly where to touch you or move his hand to a particular spot while gently encouraging, "Try this." You've been designed to enjoy a deeply erotic, completely exclusive physical love with your husband. And you are invited into the joyful journey of exploring with your husband how he can best bring *you* pleasure.

You're in the Driver's Seat

Permit me a crude comparison (I'm sorry, Mom): Have you ever been on a long car trip and needed to go to the bathroom? Have you ever noticed how easily the person driving is able to underestimate the urgency of your need? Can you relate to the frustration when the driver accidentally "forgets" that you mentioned you needed to stop about thirty minutes earlier?

Of course, great sex is about so much more than "getting relief" from a biological urge. But I believe that if you truly understand the intensity of your husband's desire for you, if you have a clear picture of what it feels like for him to sit uncomfortably forgotten in the backseat, you'll come to realize how often you are in the driver's seat.

So far in this chapter I've portrayed the husband as the initiator of sex and the wife as the resisting one. However, in the healthiest couples these roles change—with both the husband and wife initiating sex at different times. Regardless of who is pursuing and who is being pursued, though, the principle is the same: The one who has the ability to fulfill or to deny the request for intimacy is holding the power. The person in the marriage with the most power in this situation is never the one pursuing; the pursuer is, after all, the one who is risking rejection.

When you are in the driver's seat, you can make the choice to allow the sexual invitations of your husband to draw you into a mutually satisfying responsiveness. As one bride put it, "Even when I'm not in the mood, sex with my husband is almost always a good idea."

Consider one more parable: Your husband is frustrated because you constantly nag him to help out in the kitchen. The conflict over this issue gets so heated that the two of you come to talk to us. When Mark suggests that your husband may want to do a little more housework, your husband is indignant: "You're not suggesting that I need to clean the kitchen even when I don't feel like it, are you?"

By now, you probably know us well enough to know that we would say, "Yes, friend, that is *exactly* what we are suggesting."

He might argue, "But I'm just not good at kitchen cleaning. I have this built-in resistance to cleaning kitchens—

particularly when my wife seems to want me to do it all the time!"

How would you want us to respond? How about something like this: "If it matters so much to your wife that you clean the kitchen, don't make a constitutional amendment out of it. Just go clean the kitchen. In reality, by avoiding the kitchen work, you're creating much more frustration in the long run than if you simply headed straight for the sink."

Are You in the Mood?

There's a single question we pose to every couple before they get married: "Once you're married, what do you plan to do when one of you is in the mood for lovemaking and the other is not?"

If you can't come up with an answer, you're setting yourself up for a cycle in which one of you will feel pressured and the other rejected. Of course, there's no perfect strategy, no "one size fits all" answer for every couple. But our experience is that almost *any* plan works better than the all too common "Gee-whiz, I hope this works out, knock on wood" approach.

Some couples successfully use what we call the "never say no" agreement, summarized as, "If you're in the mood, I can get there." Others have an amendment to the agreement in which the pursuing partner lovingly agrees to accept a "not tonight" answer, with the understanding that it is given on a clearly limited basis. When a husband knows in advance that his wife's answer will ordinarily be yes, he's much more willing to respond with understanding than if he has the sense that "not tonight" has become the default answer.

You and your husband can come up with your own creative solutions to the pressure/rejection cycle. You may say, "This is one of those nights when I need for us to make love";

or you may ask, "Are you feeling amorous?" The key is to intentionally clarify your expectations or needs, and then agree on a plan before you end up wounding the heart of the other.

The issue is not about who gets what they want. The issue is how to use healthy sexual interest—even when it's not timed perfectly—as an opportunity for responsive intimacy rather than as a frustration that leads to resentment.

11

In-Laws: Outlaws, In-Laws, and Other Unmentionables

As far as it depends on you, live at peace with everyone.

ROMANS 12:18

———————

I met Mark when I was just fifteen years old. He was seventeen. It was 1976, and the whole country was caught up in celebrating our nation's two hundredth birthday. Our hometown of Waco, Texas, had decided to celebrate the bicentennial with a citywide production of *The Music Man,* with a cast of students from all the public schools in the city.

With a head crammed with dreams about being on stage and singing, I was, along with hundreds of others, jammed into a strange high school choir room, auditioning for roles in the musical. I could only dream of playing the part of Marion, the leading lady. Since I was only five-feet-one-inch tall, I was more likely to be cast as one of the children or as a short townsperson in the chorus.

My nervousness that night didn't prevent me from looking around the room to see how others were doing in their auditions. There was one young man who caught my eye. I thought he would be the perfect Harold Hill—the male lead. *And wouldn't it be fun,* I imagined, *to play Marion and have to kiss him for eight slow bars of music!* Little did I know that my young Harold Hill had been watching me as well.

Mark got the lead role, and, as I suspected, I got to sing in the chorus—with a one-line solo, I'm proud to say. As weeks of rehearsal turned into months, I got to know "the music man" quite well and enjoyed his rides home from rehearsal almost every night. Our routine went something like this: Go to rehearsal, take other kids home from rehearsal (did you know you can fit eight teenagers in a 1962 Volkswagen Bug?), drive to my house, sit in the car and talk—and it *was* only talk, much to my chagrin.

One night, after hours of listening to the radio with the motor turned off, Mark tried to start the car—but nothing happened. The battery was completely dead. It was after midnight, but I knew just who to call. The man who always saved me from catastrophes: my daddy. Dad was the automotive manager at the Sears store and knew more about cars than *anyone* in town. I told Mark I would just go in the house and ask Daddy to come out and help. No problem. So I did.

And did Daddy *ever* come out, looking just like, well, just like a daddy at midnight. His hair was disheveled, and he was wearing one of his vee-neck T-shirts. Topping off the look was a pair of polyester shorts. Mark got out of the car to greet him. Daddy took one disapproving look at the teenage boy who had spent the last couple hours "talking" in the dark with his daughter and asked him to get back in the car. Mark obeyed without a word. Daddy's mission was to get the car started and get his daughter into the house. Small talk with this boy was not a priority.

The plan was for Dad to push, and once the car had a little speed, Mark would pop the clutch. The engine would start, and Mark would be on his merry way. And that's exactly what happened. We lived on a hill, so Daddy didn't have to push much. The car started right up. I was beaming. The two most important men in my life had finally met, and now they had succeeded in their first project together.

I don't know how parents know these things, but a few years later, when Mark asked to marry me, Daddy told Mark that he knew—on the night of the dead battery—that Mark was going to be "the one." Three-and-a-half years later, I walked down the aisle of First United Methodist Church on my daddy's arm. When we got to the front of the church, one of the ministers popped the big question: "Who gives this woman to be married to this man?"

My father, who ordinarily kept his faith to himself, surprised us all with these words: "The Lord Jesus who gave her to us, her mother, and I do." That day he, along with our other parents, added a new title to his resume: "In-law."

In-Laws

They can be intimidating, infuriating, and intrusive, but they can also bring an incredible, incomparable stability to a marriage. In fact, in some European cultures, the low divorce rate is due, at least in part, to the presence of a supportive extended family surrounding the marriage. In-laws can be wonderful. That's the good news. But do beware: The relationship between you and your in-laws can be less than smooth and supportive. Overly involved or, conversely, overly detached parents can put stress on a marriage.

As you're getting started in your new life, it's imperative that *you and your husband*—not your parents—set the guidelines and boundaries that will be most supportive of your marriage in the long run. But get ready. Making these adjustments will most likely be more challenging for you than it will be for your husband.

A New Hero

Scott and Joan were having trouble communicating and needed an objective third party to help them sort things out. The conversation turned to the subject of her father. Her eyes lit up as she described his strength, his kindness, and his availability to them as a couple. She talked affectionately about how he had come over to trim the bushes recently—without even being asked—and how he had bought her a plane ticket so she could attend her high school reunion.

She was animated, and her voice was lively and engaging. But Scott's face revealed a different story. The more she talked in glowing terms about her father, the more Scott's countenance dropped.

"My dad is my hero," Joan said with a flourish as she finished her remarks.

At that moment, Joan might as well have pounded the mat and declared Scott down for the count. Instead of motivating her husband, her unqualified admiration for her father demoralized Scott and moved him toward nonresponsiveness and apathy.

After Bobbie and Robert were married, Bobbie and her mother talked frequently on the phone. Bobbie had grown up in a home where the act of spending money was celebrated. Now, as a newlywed, she was facing an austerity she hadn't known. The phone conversations with her mom often turned—predictably—to the subject of money. Bobbie was open about what she and Robert couldn't afford, and Bobbie's mother frequently offered to "help."

Even though you'd think Robert would have been delighted with the extra cash in the account, he wasn't. In fact, Bobbie's appreciation for "her mother's generosity" became unfair competition for her new husband. It was when Robert finally asked Bobbie to stop talking about finances with her mother that Bobbie began to realize how insecure these gifts made him feel. And as painful as it was for her to give up the goodies, Bobbie agreed.

The lesson to be learned here is this: When you compare your husband—directly or subtly—to either of your parents, your marriage loses.

With nothing but the best intentions, parents can sabotage the stability of a young marriage. When a mom or dad says to an adult daughter—with or without words—"Honey, if things don't work out, you can always come back home," seeds of marital insecurity are planted. The message is this: "You may be married to this man, but deep down we all know that you're really still ours."

More often than not, in-law challenges are caused by the good things they offer—gifts, trips, meals, baby-sitting. Unintentionally, though, these gifts can leave residual guilt and instill pressure to "perform"—to show up for the family reunion, to come for Christmas dinner, to take or not take a particular job. So naturally there will be times when you feel torn between disappointing your husband or disappointing your parents—or his.

When a choice is required, couples in the strongest marriages *choose to disappoint their parents*. They do it lovingly and respectfully. They may have to set boundaries repeatedly in order to affirm that their loyalty is to each other and that their love for and loyalty to their parents come second.

You and Your Mother-in-Law

Dealing with in-laws can be a *huge* issue, especially in the first year of marriage. And it's not a new problem. The first book of the Bible—the book of Genesis—counsels the man to step away from parents as a foundational step in building the right kind of marriage: "A man will leave his father and mother and be united to his wife, and they will become one flesh."[33]

Like many wives, you may find that your most acute in-law difficulties take place between you and your mother-in-law. Here's why: Tensions can result when both of you are vying—even subconsciously—for the affection of the same man. And if he doesn't intentionally choose to "leave," he forces his wife to compete with his mother for the rest of their lives.

This unresolved situation can hinder the building of a strong marriage:

- There is the daughter-in-law who chronically feels that, in her mother-in-law's eyes, she'll never be good enough for her son.
- There is the mother-in-law who is "concerned" that her son has changed since his marriage, and she's worried that she has "lost her son."
- There are the daughter-in-law's hypersensitive feelings—feelings so raw that anything her mother-in-law does is wrong: if she gives a gift, it's the wrong kind; if she doesn't call, she doesn't care; if she does call, she's being intrusive; if she gives money, she's being controlling; if she doesn't give money, she's being selfish.

Jason and Lynn's Nonnegotiables

By the time she and Jason decided to get married, Lynn had seen too many friends entangled in trivial, exhausting tensions with their mothers-in-law. She determined that her marriage would be different. And so, before the wedding, she and Jason developed one of the most helpful strategies for preventing in-law tension we've ever seen. After hours of discussion, they came up with these five nonnegotiables:

1. We will always speak and listen respectfully to our own parents and to each other's parents.

2. When holidays come, we will decide, without feeling guilty, where it's best for the two of us to be. Once we've decided, we'll let our parents know.

3. We will put a fair limit on our time and conversation with our parents, so that when they call or visit, we can welcome them with open arms rather than treat them as intrusive interrupters. (We don't, for example, have to answer the phone every time they call or say yes to every invitation they give.)

4. We will each agree happily to attend three in-law "command performances" each year. (Lynn might say, "Jase, if it's important to you that I go with you and your parents to the polka festival, I'll be the first one on the dance floor." And when the dancing is over, Jason recognizes that he's used up one of Lynn's command performances.)

5. We will choose our attitudes rather than blame others for our responses. (Lynn recognized

that for her to grow bitter over her relationship with her mother-in-law would never help her marriage. She determined that *she* would be the one to decide how she would respond to her mother-in-law. She told me, "I will never say to my husband, 'Your mother *made* me so angry!' I always want to be the one to *choose* my response to her.")

Jason and Lynn's strategy is a starting point. Did this plan keep Lynn from ever getting irritated with her mother-in-law? Of course not. But it did help keep her from reacting negatively or childishly when her mother-in-law hurt her feelings in some way.

If you move into your marriage without the protection of your own in-law agreement—similar to the one Lynn and Jason established—you may be setting yourselves up for years of conflict and frustration. Whether or not you think you'll ever need them, you and your husband must begin to make nonnegotiable rules of your own so that you have a plan to deal with the future. If you lay the groundwork in the first year of your life as Mr. and Mrs., it will give you a wonderful resource when and if both sets of your parents become Grandpa and Grandma.

The Tension of Time

To give couples a perspective on healthy relationships with in-laws, Mark and I try to help them gain a clear sense of *normal*—what they can expect from each other when it comes to the amount of time they'll be spending with their own families and with their in-laws. We do this by inviting couples to play a little game.

We explain that we're going to ask two questions, each of which requires a specific number for an answer. We ask them not to share their answers out loud until we signal them. When we're sure they understand the process, we ask about the bride's family: "How many days — with or without her husband — will this bride need to spend with her family (parents, grandparents, siblings, extended family) in a given year?" As they begin calculating their answers, we remind them not to speak until we give the signal. Once they have their number, we count to three, and they call out their — sometimes very different — numbers in unison. Then we ask the question about the groom's family: "How many days — with or without his wife — will this groom need to spend with his family in a given year?"

The answers are often fascinating and often quite entertaining. When, for example, the husband guesses that his bride-to-be will need to see her family twenty-four days a year, and her answer is 240 days, we know we've got something to talk about.

There is no hard-and-fast rule here. There may be times — when a parent is sick, or you or your husband work in the family business, for example — that time with parents could be unusually lengthy. Regardless of your situation, though, remember the basic principle for relating to in-laws: Decide early on to protect your marriage by disappointing your parents rather than jeopardize your marriage.

Stay Connected with Your Husband First

Sharon had a low-grade frustration about her marriage. She couldn't identify the specific problem, so she spoke in generalities about a sense of "being disconnected" from her husband. I asked questions — about time together, about their conversations, and then I asked about in-laws. Her voice danced as she talked about how well she and her husband get along with her parents. "In fact," she said, "I talk to them three or four times a day."

"Three or four times a day?" I wondered out loud.

After moving to a city hours away from her parents, Sharon had naturally made up for the infrequent face-to-face contact by multiplying phone time with them. "My mom is really my best friend," she boasted. "You don't think there's anything wrong with us talking as much as we do, do you?"

I offered, "I wonder what would happen if, for the next thirty days, you limited your conversations with your parents to four times a week." She was skeptical but agreed to try it.

Without telling her husband what she was doing, Sharon informed her parents of her decision. Her mom and dad were confused and a little hurt, but they trusted their daughter and respected her perspective.

A little over a month later, Sharon and I met again, and I was eager to hear how the experiment had gone. Ever meticulous, Sharon showed up with a couple of pages of written reflections. She wrote the following:

> The first two weeks were horrible. I was so angry with you for suggesting this assignment that several times I thought about calling you just to tell you that I was calling the whole thing off. But I stuck it out, and I learned a few things I never expected to learn—about myself, my parents, and my marriage.
>
> I kept hoping that a lightbulb would go off for Chuck—that somehow during this month he would start to understand what I really needed from him. But, steady and true as always, Chuck

wasn't changing. He continued his typical—but sometimes boring—style of communicating. And the longer I moved into this experiment, the angrier I got at him. I realized how much I was missing him. I realized how far apart I felt from him. Finally, I admitted to myself how dishonest I had been for not telling him how lonely I felt.

By the third week, I knew I had to say something to Chuck. I told him that I needed to talk. We turned off the TV. I told him how much I loved him and how much I missed him and how badly I needed something to change in our marriage.

He was dumbfounded. He had no idea I was feeling this way. Then he asked that classic "guy question": "So what do you want me to do?"

I knew I had to have something specific, so I was ready. I said, "Could we take a walk and talk for twenty minutes on the nights we're home together?" He said, "Sure," but it was that whimsical smile of his that let me know that he wanted to love me even if he didn't understand me.

I believe that *not* having the emotional security blanket of talking to my parents three or four times a day stirred up a loneliness in me that I didn't have words for before. We're not out of the woods yet, but I've decided to continue to limit my phone time with my folks to give Chuck a chance to meet some of those needs.

One of your primary tasks during the first year of your marriage is to establish a new "culture" of what is normal for the two of you. Sharon had settled into a pattern of *normal* in which her most emotionally connected conversations were with her mother and father and not with her husband. And because those conversations felt safer and much more natural, she avoided taking the risk of asking Chuck for the emotional intimacy she longed to have with him.

But, of course, in-laws aren't the only potential interruptions to your new marriage.

The Delightful Interruption: Children

Denise and Eric were more than a little excited about the arrival of their first baby. Even though it was early in their marriage, they were ready. They prepared everything they could think of — everything, that is, except their relationship.

After Denise became pregnant, Eric began to miss the "carefree" Denise. For months she suffered from a morning sickness that seemed to last twenty-four hours a day. And the thought of lovemaking only seemed to nauseate her more. On those rare days when she did feel better, her face seemed to be buried in a magazine or parenting book. From Eric's perspective, she seemed to have time and energy to do things that didn't include him — paint the nursery, keep the house immaculate, pick out curtains, shop with her mom, and watch parenting videos — but little time for him and no interest in romance.

Though he was excited about the baby, Eric began to pull back, protecting himself from feeling rejected by his bride. At times, he became defensive and harsh. Not being comfortable asking for what he needed, Eric became resigned to the notion that he had lost Denise.

"Don't get me wrong," Eric told Mark after the baby came. "I love this kid. But something is definitely missing between Denise and me. She used to be my partner, my best friend, my lover — the one I wanted to do everything with.

But now, it's like she's found another best friend. I just can't compete with a newborn!"

Let's face it. With a baby in the house, you may as well throw out the idea of "balance" in your life. Nothing can upset your equilibrium quite like having a new twenty-four-hour-a-day responsibility that refuses to fit neatly into *your* schedule.

So take care of yourself, and don't stop taking care of your marriage. If the love of your life and the vitality of your relationship are not nurtured, well, your baby won't be either. Taking care of your marriage *is* taking care of your baby. There is no single more important investment you can make in your child's future than to invest in your marriage. It is not an either/or proposition. You don't have to choose between loving your children or loving your husband. The reality is this: Kids do best in homes where the marriage is put first. Like little satellites, children orbit around the marriage. If it's unstable, the kids will spin out of orbit.

Children always change a marriage. A baby will either bring you much closer to your husband or drive a wedge between the two of you. Because of the new bond that Denise experienced with her baby, Eric got the message loud and clear: "Love is in short supply around here, and you are standing outside the circle where the real love is."

Let me tell you what your husband will be wondering when the baby comes: *Will it ever be the same between us?* The answer, of course, is "No, it never will." But it doesn't mean it has to be worse.

If the time comes for you to have children, the most powerful thing you can do is to be intentional about expressing affection and attentiveness to your husband. When he senses that there is more than enough love to go around, he will be much more attentive to you and a much happier partner with you in parenting.

A Word About Exes

Betsy and William were in our weekly marriage group. This was a second marriage for Betsy, and because she had two boys from her first marriage, she had to make regular arrangements with their father. Though she had, for the most part, gotten over her anger and hurt about the divorce, nearly every time she had to talk with her ex-husband, the familiar emotions of shame and sadness were stirred up again.

As our group talked about principles for building healthy relationships with in-laws, Betsy made an insightful observation: "You know, it seems that a lot of the same principles we've been talking about for dealing with in-laws also work for a relationship with an ex-husband." Initially, the group laughed. But we could tell from the expression on her face that Betsy wasn't kidding. You could see the question marks on the faces around the group. Mark asked, "Betsy, can you say a little more about what you mean?"

Betsy was quick to answer: "Well, first of all, the big idea we've been talking about is that we've got to be careful to make our marriage central, right? To put our best emotional energy there. With me, it's not that I feel attached to my ex-husband, it's that I can easily get caught up in such frustrating conversations with him that by the time William gets home, I'm emotionally exhausted. Sometimes I have very little patience for this man I love."

"Another thing," she went on, "is that if I can't forgive my ex for what he's done to me, I hold myself hostage to resentment and bitterness. It's just like not being able to forgive parents or in-laws. Bitterness keeps us attached to the very person we're trying to pull away from."

Not only did our group begin to see how these principles applied to in-laws and other interruptions, but Betsy's comments shed light on how forgiveness can set us free.

12
Help: The Iceberg Cometh

We seem to have focused so much on exuberant beginnings and victorious endings that we've forgotten about the slow, sometimes torturous, unraveling of God's grace that takes place in the "middle places."

SUE MONK KIDD, *WHERE THE HEART WAITS*

———◆›◈‹◆———

Mark and I could hear the shouting. From a distance we couldn't tell what was going on. But as we rounded the corner and saw cars in the parking lot, the situation became frighteningly obvious. We realized that in order to get to our car we had to walk directly toward the commotion. A tall, angry man was standing outside the passenger door of a red Volvo, screaming into the window. We couldn't help but overhear pieces of the conversation—at least enough to realize that it was his wife who was receiving the full force of his rage.

The man's anger escalated out of control, and he slammed

his fist into the side of the car. Oblivious to the fact that he had an audience, he raged on at his wife, working himself into a frenzy. In a final act of desperate frustration, he began kicking the door. By this time his wife had had enough. The car began slowly moving out of the parking lot as he commanded her to stop: "Mary, don't you drive away! Mary!"

We were dumbfounded as we watched this man in a suit and fancy dress shoes chasing the car the length of the parking lot, screaming all the while, "Mary! Mary!"

What to Do When You Need to Rebuild

In some marriages—this one, for example—the need for help is painfully and publicly obvious. But more often, marriages go flat because of long, slow leaks—not because of sudden blowouts. Sadly, couples often come for counseling only after years of inattentiveness and apathy have resulted in a crisis. Deeply ingrained levels of defensiveness and contempt are often so high that any help seems too late.

Our hope is that you will put into practice a few habits that can keep your marriage so strong that you'll never get to a point of desperation. Paying attention to the cues, knowing when you need help, and making the necessary adjustments can stop the little irritants from posing any real threat to your marriage.

But no matter how deeply you love each other right now, no matter how much you have in common, there will be times in your marriage when you'll look at this man you've married and you will simply not like him. This feeling may last for a moment, a week, or a month, but you *will* experience it. At those times you will need a rebuilding strategy, a blueprint for what to do when your marriage feels as though it's wandering down the wrong path. The advice we give to couples is this: "If at any point either one of you feels that your marriage is below the 'A' level (that's 90 percent at most schools), *that's* the time to get help."

Let's start with the good news: Rebuilding is almost always possible. But it doesn't happen accidentally, any more than my kitchen *accidentally* gets clean. Marriages are restored when couples give focused attention to a few key rebuilding strategies.

Circle the Wagons

In the nineteenth century, those who traveled west across the American frontier were prepared for danger. Whether from hostile thieves or wild animals or bad weather, wagon-train travelers had one rallying cry when facing danger: "Circle the wagons."

Single-file lines were the most efficient way to travel in a wagon train, but it was also the most vulnerable. A totally different formation was required when danger was detected. Survival depended on stopping all forward progress and moving quickly into a formation that would best protect them. In your marriage, you need to learn—and learn quickly—how to circle the wagons when the need arises. The threat may be intense and obvious—such as the discovery of an addictive behavior. Or it may be slow and subtle—a gnawing feeling that something is not right. In either case you'll need a clear, agreed-upon process for circling the wagons—a willingness to do inconvenient things for the sake of survival.

It's what Nathan and Diane did. These two outstanding young adults were both strong Christians. Early in their marriage they made a simple promise: If our marriage ever hits a crisis level, we will give first priority to restoring and protecting our marriage. Little did they know how soon that promise would be put to the test.

They had been married for a little over a year when their

world fell apart. Their problems seemed ordinary, but Diane was concerned about Nathan's long work hours and his inattentiveness to her. She signed them up for a weekend marriage conference.[34]

They checked into the hotel on Friday night, enjoyed dinner together, and went to the first session. They enjoyed the speaker and took notes so they could remember the key points. Before going to bed, they eagerly reviewed some things they agreed they'd be able to do to improve their own marriage.

But it was the Saturday morning session that turned the slow leak of Diane's concern into an explosion. In talking about the challenges faced by men, the morning speaker mentioned the threat to intimacy in marriage that Internet pornography provided. Nathan held his breath, desperately hoping that Diane wouldn't take note of the comment. But he had underestimated his wife. Back in their room, Diane asked a simple question: "Have you ever looked at pornography on your computer?"

"Uh, well, yeah, I did—once."

"Once?" she pressed, the look on Nathan's face exposing his attempt to conceal the truth.

Over the next two-and-a-half hours Nathan made a full confession of his deep involvement in cyberporn. The exposure of his mind's unfaithfulness broke Diane's heart. And her tears devastated Nathan.

"I've been trapped and unable to overcome this," Nathan poured out to his bride. "But I was more afraid of losing you if you found out, so I just kept it to myself."

This could have been the beginning of the end for their marriage, but Diane and Nathan knew what to do. Because they had a plan, they circled the wagons. Nathan drastically reduced his work responsibilities for the next few weeks. They called and made an immediate appointment with a marriage counselor. They spent the week talking about what had happened. No amount of tears or contrition from Nathan could stop Diane from expressing her hurt, her anger, and her raw feelings about the situation and about him. She didn't hold back. "You have betrayed me, and I don't *feel* like staying married to you right now," she said. "But I made a 'for better or worse" commitment—and we will work this through."

On Thursday the counselor helped Nathan and Diane to continue sorting through their crisis. He showed them how to begin the process of restoring trust and intimacy to their marriage.

The time to decide how to circle the wagons—to have a plan for what to do in a crisis—is *not* when the arrows are flying. If you and your groom have never faced a crisis, you may find it hard to believe that you will one day need help in your marriage. But right now is exactly the time for you to build your plan.

Agree right now that if there's ever a time when either of you senses the need for help, the other will agree *without question* to enter the "circle the wagons" mode. This is not a time to debate whether things are really bad enough to take this step. The fact that one of you declares the need to circle the wagons is enough.

Protect your Marriage, Bury the Weapons

Regardless of the seriousness of the issue, a crisis in your marriage can only be resolved if you are willing to lay down any weapons of destruction you may be tempted to use. The *crisis* is the enemy, not your husband.

The research evidence is conclusive: There are four specific responses that will never help your marriage.[35] So commit to protecting your marriage by burying forever these weapons that only bring destruction and never bring healing:

1. defensiveness—"Oh, so it's all *my* fault now?"
2. contempt—name-calling, cutting humor, eye-rolling that accompanies such comments as, "So what are you going to do about it, sue me?"
3. withholding of attention—the passive, nonresponsive stone wall that seeks to move to a position of power by shutting down and not responding at all
4. personal attacks—"Could you pick up your socks before you go upstairs?" becomes "You don't care about anyone but yourself, do you?"

Healthy marriages play by the rules. When you're in a conflict, negative responses only escalate the problem—and someone will get hurt. Using destructive weapons may be effective in taking your partner down and winning an argument, but the first casualty is going to be your marriage.

Feed Your Marriage

Before a crisis pays a visit to your marriage, you can fill your pantry with good things. The idea is not to seek heroic—and often unrealistic—measures, such as taking a two-week trip to Hawaii. Instead, focus on simple, doable actions that can give your marriage exactly what it needs in order to grow. These are healthy staples that are marriage-nurturing activities. You can keep them on the shelves and pick one whenever you want to strengthen and rekindle your love for each other:

- Agree to take walks together.
- Establish a date night.
- Rent a movie and snuggle on the sofa.
- When you think about your husband during the day, call him or e-mail him. Tell him how much you love him.
- Leave an "I'm thinking of you" surprise gift in his closet.

Especially during a season of healing, you'll want to focus on giving a wholehearted yes to each other as much as is humanly possible. Whether the request is for you to give your husband a warm greeting at the door or for him to pick up his dirty socks in the family room, the idea is simply to feed the marriage by intentionally and warmly responding to each other's needs.

One of the best things you can do to revitalize your relationship is to attend a marriage enrichment weekend.[36] When couples tell us, "We can't afford it," we are reminded of a divorced friend whose husband spent over $25,000 on the proceedings. While he was married, this man had been rigid and unwilling to "waste" his money on a weekend getaway with his wife once a year. In comparison, a $300 weekend is a fraction of the cost you'll pay emotionally and financially if your marriage gets off course.

Build a Support Team

If you're stuck in a negative pattern—the nagging wife/unresponsive husband; the pressured wife/rejected husband; the angry wife/passive husband; the childish wife/scornful husband—identify what you're doing. And then agree that it's something you both want to stop. And once you've stopped, you'll want to have a support team in place.

Long before the fires of frustration ever threaten to engulf your marriage, make sure you have at your fingertips more than enough resources to extinguish them. So right here and right now, in your first year of marriage, put together a team of people who will promise to stand with you on the side of your marriage—a marriage mentor couple, the pastor who married you, maybe even a professional counselor you both trust. Invite them today to be a part of your support team.

You're not looking for a group of people to be your therapists and to solve your problems. You are simply looking for people whom you trust and who can create an environment of hopefulness for you—those who will encourage you to hold on to all the right reasons you married each other in the first place.

Recognize Your Power to Change Your Husband

Three weeks after our wedding, at the ripe old ages of nineteen and twenty-one, Mark and I visited a friend's church one Sunday evening for worship. To illustrate a point—a point long since forgotten—the pastor asked a question of all the married couples in the room.

"How many of you," he asked, "can honestly say that there is nothing about your husband or wife that you would like to change?"

No one raised a hand—no one, that is, except us.

All eyes turned toward us as the pastor made his way down the aisle, carrying his microphone. Walking directly up to me, he asked, "And how long have the two of *you* been married?"

"Almost three weeks," I proudly answered. The congregation, as if on cue, erupted with laughter. We were dumbfounded and angry. *Just because so many people have accepted mediocrity in marriage,* we reasoned, *doesn't mean that we have to.*

But our anger subsided long before our first anniversary, when I began to discover "one or two" habits of Mark's that I would really like to change. What that laughing congregation knew clearly we learned slowly: Every wife, no matter how much she loves the man she has married, will, sooner or later, develop a wish list of changes she'd like to make in her husband:

- Maybe you married your husband because you loved his stability, but now there are times when you sure would like to loosen him up.
- Maybe you married him because you loved his spontaneity, but now you wish he would be more predictable and better organized.
- Maybe you were attracted to him because of his athletic physique, but now you wish he'd give up the gym more often and focus on you.
- Maybe you loved his sense of humor, but now you long for conversations that don't have a punch line.

I was wrong when I assumed that an excellent marriage meant that I'd never want to change Mark. Marriage *can* be God's most effective life-shaping force for change in a person's life. And you have the ability to be an agent of change in your husband's life. But to do so, you have to come to two paradoxical realizations:

- I *cannot* change my husband.
- I really *can* change my husband.

It *is* a strange paradox. If you focus on changing your husband, you have virtually no chance of changing him. Here's why:

When a husband becomes his wife's number one home improvement project, she winds up with a man who feels powerless ever to satisfy her. He assumes that, no matter what he does, no matter how hard he tries, his wife will always be able to find one more thing about him that needs changing.

At this point, you may be thinking, *Wait just a second. I thought you told me my husband was never going to get it on his own—that I need to learn to ask for what I need from him.* Don't be confused: asking for what you need is very different from giving advice. Overloading your husband with advice and suggestions *will* be perceived as criticism, and criticism robs him of the adventure and fun he experiences in his choosing to do the noble thing—not because he was forced to do it, but because he loves you. But if he feels emasculated and dependent, it's highly unlikely that he'll make the changes you desire.

What Time Is It?

There was something I was determined to change in Mark. He had one habitual pattern that, more than any other, had irritated and angered me. More evenings than not, he was late getting home. For years I tried to change the pattern. I tried confronting him, withholding affection, scowling through dinners—all the things we've just told you not to do—but nothing seemed to work, until I ambushed him.

For the sake of fairness, I'll let Mark tell the story:

> I had tried. I really had. I set my watch ahead. I said I'd be home later than I expected to be, just to give myself some wiggle room. I got up from my chair to leave early. But my best-laid plans fell victim to the apparent conspiracy of people who just *had* to talk to me—urgently—just before I

walked out the office door. I would usually make the obligatory "I'm going to be late, honey," call and then head to the car, spending the ten-minute drive home preparing my defense.

I would say to myself. *Hey, I'm not all that bad. I'm just fifteen minutes late. I know I'm not perfect, but I'm a heck of a lot better husband than a lot of guys. And besides, this person really needed my help. His marriage was in trouble!*

By the time I got home, dinner was not the only thing that was boiling in the kitchen. I would give a halfhearted apology—an explanation, really, of whose fault it was this time. My bride would let me know how it felt not to be able to trust her husband's word; I would call a foul, and we'd have a side order of tension with our dinner.

After ten years of dealing with my habitual lateness, my wife had had it. She was tired of making the same speeches week in and week out. She was tired of trying to change my behavior. She was *really* tired of my excuses. So, like a desperate woman, she took action. Without consulting me, she decided to try something very, very different the next time I came home late—of course, she didn't have to wait long. I walked in as usual, with my rationalizations fully prepared. But I was stepping into an ambush.

Instead of the usual quiet but tense "you're late!" reception I'd grown accustomed to, I was mauled at the door by my bride. She wrapped me in a bear hug and gave a promising kiss on the lips. As she held me, she whispered in my ear, "I'm so glad you're home. I missed you so much!"

That was eight or ten years ago, I don't quite remember. What I *do* remember, though, are the changes that took place in our marriage because of the changes my bride made:

1. I don't prepare speeches or rationalizations when I *am* late.
2. I can't wait to get home.
3. When we eat together after I'm late, we still enjoy ourselves.

Does Mark still arrive home late on occasion? Sure. But there's no longer a scolding "mother" waiting for him. Now he's been motivated to change—not because of my speeches, but because he was wooed, even seduced, into change. Guess which approach he likes best.

The change happened, not just in Mark's behavior but in our marriage, when I took the focus off what I couldn't control—his lateness—and put it into what I could—my *response*.

Changing your response doesn't *guarantee* a changed husband, of course, any more than planting seeds in the ground and watering them guarantees a healthy garden. But it greatly improves your chances for a bountiful harvest. You really *can* change your husband. It happens when you go first and create an atmosphere in which transformation can happen—first in yourself, and then in your husband.

Notes

1. "What Happens after the Wedding?" Interview with Pamela Paul, Sheryl Nissinen, and Terry Real (*The Oprah Winfrey Show,* air date: 28 October 2002).

2. Leah Heidenrich, in her master's research project titled "Bride Illusion: Depression in Newlywed Women," cited in Sheryl Nissinen, *The Conscious Bride* (Oakland, Calif.: New Harbinger, 2000), 176.

3. Reported in John M. Gottman, *The Seven Principles for Making Marriage Work* (Three Rivers, Michigan: Three Rivers Press, 2000), 5.

4. Reported in Linda J. Waite and Maggie Gallagher, *The Case for Marriage: Why Married People Are Happier, Healthier, and Better-Off Financially* (New York: Doubleday, 2000), 67.

5. Ibid.

6. Reported in Philip Yancey, *Finding God in Unexpected Places* (Nashville: Moorings, 1995), 82.

7. Neil Clark Warren, *Catching the Rhythm of Love* (Nashville: Nelson, 2000), 16–17.

8. Willard F. Harley, *His Needs, Her Needs* (Grand Rapids: Revell, 1993; revised edition 2001), 7.

9. See the real-life examples in Les and Leslie Parrott, *Becoming Soul Mates* (Grand Rapids: Zondervan, 1995).

10. "The Good Wife's Guide," *Housekeeping Monthly,* 13 May 1955; can be viewed on the Internet at www.lucaschristian.com/wifeguide.htm.

11. Research cited in *CBMW News,* vol. 1, no. 3 (June 1996), 1.

12. Genesis 2:18.

13. Many of the foundational principles in this chapter have been inspired by John Eldredge's treatment of this topic in *Wild at Heart*(Nashville: Nelson, 2001).

14. Genesis 4:1, emphasis added.

15. Psalm 27:9, emphasis added.

16. See John 14:16, 26; 15:26; 16:7.

17. The National Domestic Violence Hotline (1-800-799-SAFE [7233]) is staffed twenty-four hours a day to provide crisis assistance and information related to spouse abuse.

18. C. S. Lewis, *That Hideous Strength* (New York: Macmillan, 1946), 76.

19. Quentin Schultze, *Winning Your Kids Back From the Media* (Downers Grove, Ill.: InterVarsity Press, 1994), 30.

20. Jane Austen, *Sense and Sensibility* (New York: Bantam Books, 1983), 316.

21. Story adapted from Gary Smalley, *The Hidden Value of a Man* (Colorado Springs: Focus on the Family, 1992), 106.

22. Dialogue adapted from Jeff Van Vonderen, *Families Where Grace Is in Place* (Minneapolis: Bethany House, 1992), 49–50.

23. Gottman, *Seven Principles for Making Marriage Work*, 17, 20.

24. Ibid., 79.

25. Ibid., 264.

26. Ibid., 177.

27. Ibid., 114.

28. Ibid., 179.

29. Ibid., 130.

30. Richard Swenson, *Margin* (Colorado Springs: NavPress, 1995), 168.

31. Cited in Mary Pipher, *The Shelter of Each Other* (New York: Ballantine, 1996), 38.

32. For more information about healing from sexual abuse, see Lynn Heitritter and Jeanette Vought, *Helping Victims of Sexual Abuse* (Minneapolis: Bethany House, 1989); also visit www.joshua childrensfoundation.org.

33. Genesis 2:24.

34. Diane signed up for a "Family Life Today" conference. Find out more about this organization on the Internet at www.familylife.com.

35. See Gottman, *Seven Principles for Making Marriage Work*, 27.

36. Marriage Encounter (1-800-795-LOVE); Marriage Enrichment (1-800-634-8325); A Weekend to Remember (501-223-8663).

Couples of the Bible

A One-Year Devotional Study of Couples in Scripture

Robert and Bobbie Wolgemuth

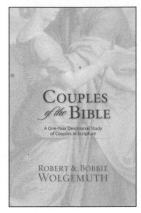

In this scrapbook of your spiritual family tree faithful patriarchs and matriarchs who make you proud . . . and scoundrels you'd rather not talk about. But all of these couples of the Bible will give you a instructive snapshot of your biblical heritage. Some bring encouragement; others offer a stern warning.

Through this 52-week devotional experience, you will be reacquainted with the challenges and outcomes of familiar couples such as Abraham and Sarah . . . and meet some lesser-known couples such as Othniel and Aksah. Each week focuses on one couple, from Adam and Eve to Christ and His Bride. You will read their story, learn about their cultural setting, and explore how their story can teach important truths about your own marriage. You will be guided with questions to help you apply biblical truth to your relationship with your spouse. And you'll finish the week with a time of reflection, thanksgiving, and prayer.

Couples of the Bible will teach you how God guided couples in the past and will encourage you to trust in his faithfulness for your marriage both in the present and in the future.

Men of the Bible

A One-Year Devotional Study of Men in Scripture

*Ann Spangler and
Robert Wolgemuth*

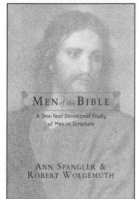

Men of the Bible offers both men and women a fresh way to read and understand the Bible—through the eyes and hearts of the men whose stories unfold in its pages. This unique book takes a close-up look at fifty-two men in Scripture whose dramatic life stories provide a fresh perspective on the unfolding story of redemption.

Though our culture differs vastly from theirs, the fundamental issues we face remain the same. We still reach for great dreams and selfish ambitions. We wrestle with fear and indecision and experience the ache of loneliness and the devastation of betrayal. And, like many of these men, we long to walk more closely with the God who calls us into an intimate relationship with himself.

In *Men of the Bible*, each week becomes a personal retreat focused on the life of a particular man: His Story—a narrative retelling of the biblical story; A Look at the Man—focusing on the heart of the man and how his story connects with your own life; His Legacy in Scripture—a short Bible study on principles revealed through his life; His Legacy of Promise—Bible promises that apply to his life and yours; His Legacy of Prayer—praying in the light of his story.

Women of the Bible

A One-Year Devotional Study of Women in Scripture

Ann Spangler and Jean E. Syswerda

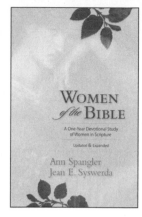

Women of the Bible, by Ann Spangler and Jean E. Syswerda, focuses on fifty-two remarkable women in Scripture—women whose struggles to live with faith and courage are not unlike your own. The women in this book encourage you through their failures as well as their successes.

Women of the Bible offers a unique devotional experience that combines five elements. Each week becomes a personal retreat focused on the life of a particular woman: Her Story—a moving portrait of her life; Her Life and Times—background information about the culture of her day; Her Legacy in Scripture—a short Bible study on her life; Her Promise—Bible promises that apply to her life and yours; Her Legacy of Prayer—praying in the light of her story.

Special features include a list of all the women of the Bible, a timeline of the women of the Bible, a list of women in Jesus' family tree, and a list of women in Jesus' life and ministry

This yearlong devotional will help you slow down and savor the story of God's unrelenting love for his people, offering a fresh perspective that will nourish and strengthen your personal communion with him.

Share Your Thoughts

With the Author: Your comments will be forwarded to the author when you send them to *zauthor@zondervan.com*.

With Zondervan: Submit your review of this book by writing to *zreview@zondervan.com*.

Free Online Resources at
www.zondervan.com

Zondervan AuthorTracker: Be notified whenever your favorite authors publish new books, go on tour, or post an update about what's happening in their lives at www.zondervan.com/authortracker.

Daily Bible Verses and Devotions: Enrich your life with daily Bible verses or devotions that help you start every morning focused on God. Visit www.zondervan.com/newsletters.

Free Email Publications: Sign up for newsletters on Christian living, academic resources, church ministry, fiction, children's resources, and more. Visit www.zondervan.com/newsletters.

Zondervan Bible Search: Find and compare Bible passages in a variety of translations at www.zondervanbiblesearch.com.

Other Benefits: Register yourself to receive online benefits like coupons and special offers, or to participate in research.